Leadership Insights

Leadership Insights

11 Typical Mistakes Young Leaders Make and Tips to Avoid Them

Matt L. Beadle

BEP BUSINESS EXPERT PRESS

Leadership Insights: 11 Typical Mistakes Young Leaders Make and Tips to Avoid Them

First published in 2019 by
Business Expert Press, LLC
222 East 46th Street, New York, NY 10017
www.businessexpertpress.com

ISBN-13: 978-1-94819-827-1 (paperback)
ISBN-13: 978-1-94819-828-8 (e-book)

Business Expert Press Human Resource Management and Organizational Behavior Collection

Collection ISSN: 1946-5637 (print)
Collection ISSN: 1946-5645 (electronic)

Cover and interior design by Exeter Premedia Services Private Ltd., Chennai, India

First edition: 2019

10 9 8 7 6 5 4 3 2 1

Printed in the United States of America.

All diagrammes illustrated by Matt Beadle

Abstract

Leading ones first team can be a daunting and sometimes overwhelming experience, requiring self-reflection, self-discipline, communication, and organizational skills, as well as no small amount of guts and values. This book provides young leaders or future high-potentials the guidance needed on how to deal with the challenges of leading teams in modern organizations.

Understanding the power of strengths-based leadership using clear two-way communication and, in particular, identifying with one's own leadership philosophy are central themes in this book. It highlights the typical mistakes made by first-time leaders and offers theoretical and practical advice to deal with the difficulties of management.

Keywords

communication; first team lead; leadership values; leadership; management; persuasion; positive psychology; self-development; self-management; self-reflection; strengths-based leadership

Contents

Foreword

About 10 years ago, at the height of running my former company, things were good. We had a large, content, growing customer base, which ranged SMEs right up to global players. I had many people working for me and with me, and I felt like the king of the castle. This thing that I had started on my own from my basement had spawned into a successful company with good profit margins, high turnover, no debt, significant assets, a sound reputation, happy team members, and satisfied clients.

I was not only proud of the company's KPIs, I was very proud of the feedback I received from the vast majority of people with whom I worked. They enjoyed their work and felt inspired and motivated that they were part of something. We were not just buying something for a dollar and selling it for two, we offered services, which helped our customers, and we were content with the quality we added.

It was then that I was overjoyed to win a large, new client. I had been lucky enough to have my company recommended by an existing, happy client, and after the pitch process was successful, we made all the arrangements and set up the project. The client was based in a region we had not yet broken into, and so I did what I had done many times before: I searched for a project manager whom I would employ on a contractual consultancy basis to head up the new project and see to the client's needs. I found someone whom I deemed suitable. His credentials and experience seemed excellent. Just what I was looking for. I interviewed him personally, invited him out for a nice meal, and welcomed him into the team.

The project for the client began, and that is when things started to go awry. My project manager (we will call him Ivan) very quickly became elusive. He seemed to be avoiding my calls, did not report in at the intervals that we had discussed and had not asked for any budgetary support or materials, which he would normally need for such a project.

After a considerable amount of sleuthing on my part, it turned out that Ivan had completely ripped me off. He had introduced himself to my new client and presented a letter, which he claimed was from me, in which it stated that the project would be run solely by *his* company on my corporation's behalf. Put simply: he deceitfully stole my newest, biggest client. By the time the client had discovered the lies, they had already committed legally to Ivan's company. They apologized personally and profusely for their (inadvertent) part in the whole debacle, but their hands were now tied.

I finally reached Ivan on the phone, and desperate for an explanation, I grilled him for answers. When I was finished, he laughed sarcastically, said:

Matt, you are an amateur!

and hung up the phone.

Probably, the lowest point in my managerial career, I reflected deeply upon the mistakes I had made. I had not signed a contract with Ivan. I had never signed contracts up to that point, in fact, with any of my consultants or joint venture partners. Indeed, I had not even signed contracts with many of my customers. I had built a company and reputation based on mutual trust, and it had backfired on me painfully. I made myself a promise that day, listening to the beeping at the end of the telephone:

I would stick to my leadership values as a leader now, more than ever.

I had never signed a contract with partners before Ivan, and I never did so after Ivan! I continued to run my company for many years in exactly the same way in which I had before Ivan had defrauded me and called me an amateur. I worked with people, developed relationships, built mutual trust, explained the why, and led strengths-oriented, transformationally, and transparently. In fact, at the next opportunity, I wrote down my leadership values in my own version of a *leadership compass* (see Chapter 12) and led by them proudly and successfully for another 10 years—indeed, many of those musings have, organically, become the foci of this book.

I had realized that day what business is. Business is not contracts, products, services, processes, spreadsheets, meetings, pitches, supply chains, or KPIs. The only thing that absolutely all professional organizations in the whole world have in common is: people. As of 2018, every corporation on this planet (still) has people at its core, producing and selling its products or providing its services.

During my nearly 20 years founding and running my own company, heading up a faculty at a university, lecturing undergrad and graduate students in team and communication, and delivering leadership workshops to tens of thousands of professionals across a host of industries, and in many countries, my assertion has been confirmed again and again.

Business is people.

This book is not about contracts or whether or not one should sign them. This is not a list of rights or wrongs in business or how a good leader should or should not act. This book is about helping you establish what is important to you in your leadership experience.

This book is about the value of values.

It is not a collection of leadership recommendations, to-dos, or self-help advice. It is not a quick win and might leave you with more new questions than it provides answers.

In the following pages, I hope to give you a kick-start on your life-long journey of self-reflection toward becoming the inspirational leader you would like to and deserve to become. This book is the culmination of my two decades of experience in and musings on this fascinating subject of leadership. It is the critical mass of my professional work, and I hope you each find at least one take-home. I would love that.

Acknowledgments

I have had the pleasure to have worked with and be inspired by so many wonderfully gifted intellectuals before and during my pulsating career, and I would like to thank all those who contributed small and large to my professional development over the years. In no particular order, thank you to the following people without whom I would not have ever come to develop the professional experience or knowledge needed to write this book. Claudia Ott, Prof. Frau Dreier, Dr. Jochem Kießling-Sonntag, Marion Schopen, Dr. Klaudia Fork, Markus Rempe, Prof. Dr. Gerhard Klippstein, Prof. Dr. Volker Wittberg, Christian Ott, Daniel Klarhorst, Jo Gordon, Beth Hinton, Dr. Ausberto Torres, Marc Pavey, Verena Hanke-Neuland, Christian Ott, Dale Heffron, Peter Chisholm MBE, Mr. Travett, Britta Landermann, Rita Mintert, Jens Ott, Guido Neuland, Michael Tulipan, the employee at the job center, Detlef Dammeier, Zoran Nikolic, Sören Heidemann, Miron Tadic, Glynn Turner, Denise Bickert, and the guy who escorted me to the train in Bremen. Special thanks to Adam Orchard for teaching me how to say "my mother is a budgerigar". Thanks to Fernando M., Aldo O., and Nancy S. for kindly letting me use their leadership compass collages.

To my mentor and hoser Christiaan Lorenzen, I give particular thanks. Your ceaseless advice at the beginning of my career in management training was invaluable, and I feel hugely in your debt. I thank Dr. Phillipa Ward for teaching me how to chain logic together and structure argumentation and for convincing me that even a jock is allowed to sit at the intellectuals' table.

My dear friends (and their families), spread across the world, steadfastly gave me the self-belief to follow my star, no matter how badly I nurse our relationships. Thank you boys! Chris Jones, James Laing, Arron Edwards, Björn Herbath, John Carr, Neil Clarke, Peter Hill, Stuart and Andy Henderson, and Chris Rayment.

I am hugely grateful to my two trainer hotshot friends Gabor Holch and Klaus Dürrbeck for their great help with editing, consulting, and tweaking, in particular, the chapter on the brain. My thanks to Nigel Whyatt for first approaching me about writing this book and to Rob Zwettler at BEP for publishing it. The collaboration has been a pleasure, and I hope it is not our last.

My thanks go out to all of my colleagues at SYNK Group, in particular Eva Hönnecke, Uli Moehler, David Liebnau, Dr. Martin Friedrich, Christine Ait-Mohktar, Lutz Pickhardt, and Udo Krauss. Your faith in me and the collaboration with you on myriad projects over the years has been a great honor and has helped me develop as a consultant immensely.

To all my colleagues at the Munich Leadership Group, led by the inspirational Dr. Paul Schurmann and Dr. Hans-Werner Hagemann, and in particular Michael Knieling, Doreen Koehler, Natalie Rosengart, Stephanie Jagdhuber, and Anja Wiendl, I say thank you for your belief and motivation and for the dynamic, transformational way you run your company and serve your clients.

My endless love and thanks go to my mum and dad and to my brothers, Richard and Jack, who brought me up in an environment drowned with words, and at the same time, taught me how to swim. Thank you Emily and Lenny for reminding me of the *why*, every day. You are the reason I do everything I do.

My final thanks go to my raison d'etre, my muse, my dearest friend, and the most selfless listener I have ever met. You are an extraordinary woman, and I thank you from the bottom of my heart for every iota of support you have ever given me.

For GB

CHAPTER 1

Do You Want to Drive the Bus?

Leaders Often Underestimate Leadership

200 Souls

The year was 1945. My grandfather, together with millions like him, returned home from the war to a bleak welcome. His family's house in South East London had been extensively damaged in the war. My father and aunt (then just children) and my grandmother were in dire need of warmth, nourishment, and a roof over their heads. The arrangement in those days was that everyone returning from the front had the right to take up the job that he or she had held before the war, but unfortunately, my grandfather's former employer no longer existed. It had been razed to the ground during the Blitz. Without the safety net of a social welfare system (such support was years off), my grandfather's position was precarious, and it was obvious: his family's mere survival depended upon him finding employment–and fast.

He applied, it is said, for hundreds of jobs. It was not that he was not employable. He had skills, experience, and no end of drive, but he was not alone. There were literally hundreds of thousands like him searching for and applying for the same positions. In such a saturated market, standing out from the crowd can prove very difficult. Nevertheless, eventually, he returned home one day with the news that he had been offered a job. My grandmother, whom I sadly only had the pleasure to know briefly while I was a small child, was apparently a woman of few words. Family lore says that she was only known to show her emotions on a couple of occasions in her life. The day my grandfather came home with the job offer was one of those times.

My grandmother danced around the front room with the children, smiling across her face as she sang, *We're saved ... everything is going to be alright ... Daddy has a job....* However, my grandfather did not have a job. He had indeed been *offered* a position to work as a London bus driver, but he had turned down the offer. He had not taken the job.

Apparently, that was the second time in her life that my grandmother showed her emotions.

With sheer consternation, she harangued my grandfather for what she viewed as an awful decision. How could he turn down such a job offer, such a gift? How could he put his family's welfare on the line with such a decision? She pleaded. My grandfather, whom I never met as he sadly died before I was born, solemnly responded to his wife's vociferous appeals:

Darling, I turned down the job, because I did not want the responsibility of 200 souls on my bus.

After much consideration, I, personally have come to the firm conclusion that I am hugely impressed by my grandfather's decision. He had the strength of conviction to make such a difficult decision despite acute awareness of the potential ramifications for others (his family). He put his values before potential material gain when he decided that he did not want to bear such a large responsibility. Some may see such a move as cowardly or feeble, but not I. For me, he had reflected on and made the most important and wide-ranging decision a professional can make, namely:

Do I want to take on the responsibility?

Leaders bear the burden of responsibility, irrespective of industry. In my nearly two decades as a management consultant and coach, I have unfortunately heard regret expressed by hundreds of leaders, from many different industries.

Sometimes, I wish I had never become a manager! This is not what I had thought it would be like...I am not cut out for this...I wish I had more time for my family...I take these issues home with me...it consumes me...being a leader has made me ill. Et cetera.

My message here is not that leadership and management are solely bad stars to follow and should not be recommended as career paths. On the contrary, leadership can be powerful, exciting, stimulating, and hugely rewarding. Leaders have the chance to make a difference.

The message here is that leadership is not for everyone.

Maybe you are just embarking on your professional career, maybe you are looking forward to imminent promotion to your first leadership role, or maybe you are already in such a role. Wherever you currently find yourself on your professional or leadership journey, I implore you to seriously self-reflect and ask yourself whether you truly want the responsibility and all the trappings and challenges that come with leadership. Before you read the rest of this book, you should be able to honestly answer the question:

Do I want to drive the bus?

Would You Push the Big Guy?

There is an exercise that psychology professors sometimes run with their first semester undergrads:

Imagine you are casually going for a walk, minding your own business when you hear the sound of a train in the distance. You turn, and from your position, you can see the train fast approaching. Suddenly, your attention is piqued by a group of youths (seven or eight of them) playing on and near the track (Figure 1.1). They appear to be oblivious to the approaching locomotive. You call out to them to move, but they cannot hear you. Just as you are calculating whether or not you will have the time to run to them to warn them yourself (you will not), you notice that you are standing next to the controls that switch the points. If you were to switch the points, the train would follow the side track and the youths would be saved.

In a freakishly similar situation, you find yourself, days later, by another train track. You again witness 7 to 8 people dangerously on or by the rain track (Figure 1.2). A train is fast approaching and will surely kill them all. They cannot hear you. You cannot make it to them fast enough. But, you can switch the points. However, there is a young child on the side track, on the track that you would divert the train to, if you switched

Figure 1.1 Would you switch the points?

the points. You cannot warn or reach either the lone girl or the group of youths. What will you do?

Figure 1.2 Would you switch the points?

Days later (you seem to be having some bad luck on your walks in the country), you find yourself in the same situation again (Figure 1.3). The same as before, but in this case, the single person on the side track is someone very dear to you (for example your mother, partner, or sibling).

Figure 1.3 Would you switch the points?

Several days later (déjà vu?) you have decided to change your route through the woods, and instead wander along the top of the hill, over-looking the train track (Figure 1.4). Tragically, you witness a similar situation: a group of people is playing on the track, but this time, you cannot reach the controls to the points in time. You cannot verbally or physically warn the kids that the train is coming. Their fate appears doomed. However, near you, you see a huge man. He must be nearly seven-feet tall and weigh several hundred pounds. He is a powerhouse of a man. Strong, ripped, massive. You quickly surmise that, if you were to push the man from his vantage point on the hill, he would fall in front of the train causing the driver to brake or his large body would slow the speed of the train enough to save the loitering teenagers.

Would you push the big guy?

Admittedly, the preceding situations are extreme. Let us hope neither you nor I nor anyone we know is faced with such intense dilemmas. But, the truth remains that, were we to find ourselves in such high-pressure scenarios, we would have to make a decision. One way or the other.

Reacting to the previous scenarios, almost all subjects asked, choose to switch the points to divert the train to the side track in the first example. When asked, most respond that they would intervene if they felt that their actions could benefit the group. Only a small percentage of respondents say that they would do nothing at all. Indeed, I have also run the example with numerous groups myself, and one or two over the years have answered thus: It was their stupid decision to sit near a train track, so why should I get involved in their lives.

But, the vast majority chose to switch the points. When faced with the second of the dilemmas (1.2.2), the majority, also here, claim that they would switch the points. The most common defense of their actions sounds something like this:

If I were forced to make such a decision, I would choose to save the *many* over saving the *one*. Seven lives are more valuable than one.

Interestingly, the water is muddied considerably when people are asked how they would act in situation 1.2.3. The most still choose to save the many over the one, but a not-insignificant minority state that they would save their loved one and let the train kill the group. I have asked this question of thousands of workshop participants, and many chose to leave the points as they were in favor of their family member. Indeed, in some groups, more than half decided in that way. It appears that blood is, indeed, at times, thicker than water and that—contrary to the statements to 1.2.2—sometimes several lives are, in fact, *not* more important than one. Even more interestingly, subjects in this study often change their mind again and choose to switch to save the youths after all, when they are faced with the knowledge that their loved one on the side track is very old or terminally ill.

When responding to whether or not they would push the big guy, the most do not. They argue that he is not even involved. He is minding his own business and so should not have to die to save the youths. It would be unfair for to sacrifice him as he has done nothing wrong. Here, the *several-lives-are-more-valuable-than-one* argument also does not seem to apply. When asked to reflect on this situation, many state that it is different from 1.2.2 or even 1.2.3 because the people on the side track in those situations *chose* to be involved. They chose to sit in a dangerous spot. The big guy chose not to be involved and so, should get a pass. Some do choose to push the big guy to save the many, but in my experience, such a choice is rare. Leaving the matter of what may or may not be legal in any particular jurisdiction in those situations to one side for the moment, let us look at the forces at play, when we have to make such momentous decisions. These decisions (and many we make) are based on our values.

Our journey through life, our upbringing, the culture(s) we have lived in, the people we have met, and the experience we have made, even the languages we speak (Pinker 2003), these influences and many more mold our personal values. These values, often referred to as our *internal compass* or as *common sense* are, in fact, not common at all. Our values are unique to us. Each of us will have differing views and instincts depending upon the complexity of any given situation. Your challenge as a leader is to tap into these instincts, listen to and understand your inner voice, and then translate your values into action, decisions, and judgments.

In the preceding example, maybe you sacrificed the (one) child to save the (many) youths. Maybe this *many-lives-are-more-precious-than-one* equation was rejected when the one was your mother or brother. Maybe you did not push the big guy because he had not done anything wrong. After all, the child was stupid enough to play on the tracks in the first place. Or maybe, you pushed the big guy to save the many.

Leaders have to make difficult decisions every day. Fact. Should we hire the less-qualified single father of three or the better-qualified university graduate? Should we build that plant next to the river? Should we recall millions of products and suffer huge losses because one box contained a shard of plastic? Should I fire the employee who broke company rules and was in breach of his or her contract, although he or she happens to be a dear friend? Shall we make those 300 people redundant to remain profitable and able to employ the other 900? Should I, as a leader, stand up for my team, against the wishes of my own superior, and in doing so, risk my own job security? Should I choose to delegate the awful task or carry it out myself although I have neither the time nor the inclination?

Leadership can be extremely challenging, and it is hugely important to me that you have reflected on this deeply, before you enter into management. Leadership involves making difficult decisions, and these decisions will be based on your values and strengths. I invite you to reflect on what is important to you; on what your values are.

Driving the bus can be immensely rewarding. You get to choose the route and speed of travel. However, wanting to remain a passenger is absolutely no disgrace. Taking the bus on your journey is fine. Indeed, having others drive you can be positively pleasurable at times.

You alone can, and should, decide. Do you want to drive the bus?

You Are Here

When I was a child, my parents used to take my brothers and me to the zoo. I remember one time, the air conditioning in our car was broken, and so we had to drive through the safari park melting in 35 degree heat while the monkeys ripped the car to shreds. Lambs to the slaughter. Either way, the color and tone of the zoo always fascinated me. The myriad creatures with their different habitat and dietary demands, also. The zoo's employees whose role is to create as comfortable an environment for their animals as possible while, at the same time, building a suitable ambiance for their customers, the visiting public. I loved visiting the zoo.

Moreover, one thing always struck me when I entered a zoo or a safari park. The first thing one sees when one enters such a park is a large board with a map on it (Figure 1.4). It shows you where all the animals can be

Figure 1.4 Zoo map: you are here

found. The elephants are at the back of the park, the penguins are just round the first corner, the lions are on the right side, and so on. Oh, and it, of course, showed us exactly where the overly priced gift shop was. At the bottom of the sign, though, there was always a large red dot and with an arrow pointing to it together with the label: "You are here."

That red point allowed you to get your bearings. It allows you to appreciate where you are in relation to other attractions, and some people find that they *save* a rough picture of that map in their minds while traveling through the zoo and recall it at will to help them guide themselves, all the time, referring back to that point: "You are here."

Okay. Now, save that thought, and we will return to it in a moment.

Next, if you work for an organization, think of that company's structure. If you are thinking of joining a particular company to be a leader in the future, then think of that corporation.

Now, think of the following numbers for me. If you like, write them down on the largest piece of paper or whiteboard you can find:

- How many people work, in total, for your company?
- How many of the employees at your company are in leadership positions?

What kind of numbers have you written down? If it is a large company, maybe 10,000 of its 120,000 staff are managers or leaders. If it is a smaller company, maybe those numbers are around 50 of 300. Maybe you have other numbers (Figure 1.5).

Whichever two numbers you are now looking at, draw a big, fat circle around the smaller one, that is, the number of people who currently fulfill a leadership role at your company. *You are here!*

You are a member of the elite party of leaders in that corporation. You are the *they* that people talk about (usually when complaining that change is not possible or things are not as we would like them):

"*They* (the managers of this company) have created a culture of pressure, here."

"*They* will not listen to us, even if we spoke up."

"I would love to change things around here, but *they* will not let it happen."

~*120,000*

~ *10,000*

⇧

YOU ARE HERE

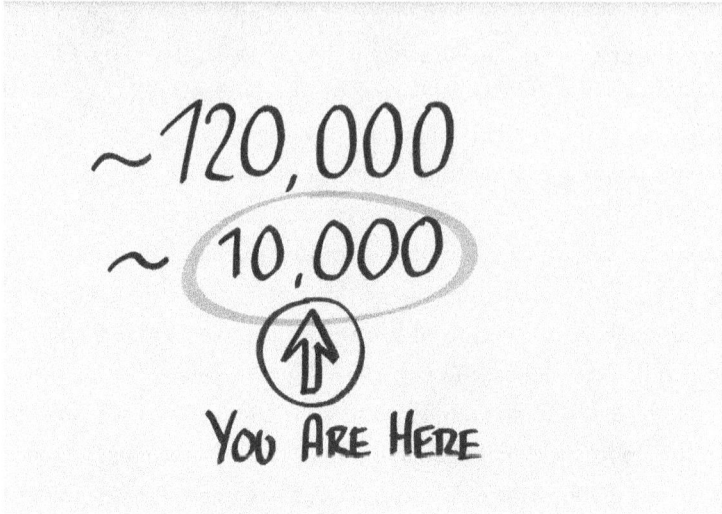

Figure 1.5 Even junior leaders are part of the they

If you are a manager, you are part of the *they*, already. Even if you are not yet in a leadership position, but consider that your aim, then, one day, you will be one of the infamous *they* too. *They* are not some mystical, untouchable, unapproachable group of ghouls. They exist, and as a leader, you are one of them. In other words, both your mindset and your language should change as soon as you take on your first leadership position. You are no longer able to blame others for the woes and weaknesses in your corporation. As a leader, you also no longer have the chance to pass the buck to others who should make the challenging decision in your stead. In the following chapters, we will look at more specific leadership situations and reflect on the best course of action to avoid the most common leadership pitfalls. However, before we do so, we need to digest the generic, fundamentals mentioned. Do you want the responsibility of leading a team? Do you know what is important to you as a leader? Have you reflected on your values, and how they will influence your decision-making? Are you prepared to make big decisions? What decisions would you make in different, precarious situations? Have you yet arrived at the mindset that, as a member of corporation management, you are part of the *they* that people talk about? As a leader, you have the exciting chance to steer the bus or at least be involved in the steering, but you will have to make some big, tough decisions along the way.

Chapter Leadership Challenge

Take a piece of paper and a pen and write the words *my values* in the middle of the page. Circle that phrase (Figure 1.6). Now, take your time, reflect deeply and add to the page, round the center words, everything that is important to you and is guided by your inner compass. Where do you stand on the train dilemmas, for example? What are your values regarding difficult employment and recruitment scenarios? How do you feel about delegating, taking on tasks you do not like, discussing sensitive information, disciplining staff members, and on all the other management settings you can think of? Use this mindmap to develop a collection of your own values. Use this list to decide if you would like to drive the bus (and how big your bus should be) and keep it with you on your journey and refer back to it periodically.

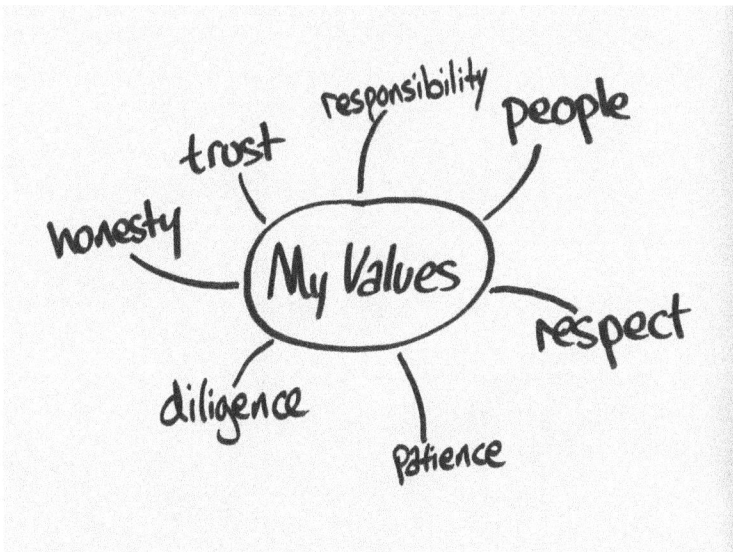

Figure 1.6 An example of a leadership value mindmap

CHAPTER 2

Start with the Why

Leaders Micromanage and Focus on Details

The Golden Circle

It is own-up time. I never used to like to read. I know that may seem strange for a linguistics graduate, former owner of a communications agency, and author of several books, but I promise, in the past, I found it hard to focus on intellectual reading unless I felt I *had to*. At school or for my college degrees, I begrudgingly picked up the literature on my teachers' and lecturers' recommended reading lists, but I painfully struggled, unmotivated through those works and only because faculty had told me what to read. My university lecturers sounded something like this:

"In semester 1 Jones, Edwards, and Carr are compulsory reading, and make sure you have read Laing and Brownbridge and Clarke, Henderson and Hill by the end of semester 2…"

Years later, during the first stages of my career as a management trainer, I was lucky enough to have worked on successful training projects and felt that, if the last client was happy, then the next one also would be. I felt confident of my abilities and I felt little need to *go back to the books,* certainly not to the ones that my lecturers had forced me to read at university. However, around the same time, I began to have the benefit of tandem training with a number of renowned, highly experienced, and gifted management consultants. I loved to watch them, learn from them, and tried to soak up their techniques and tidbits of knowledge. I was inspired by them. One thing that they all had in common is that they all read *all the time*! All my trainer colleagues ever seemed to talk about was this book or that author. They were an inspiration to watch deliver their workshops, and they soaked up the contents of subject literature like sponges and then suddenly, I saw the connection. I saw the reason to read.

If I too were to read as they read and read what they read, then maybe I, too, would be able to train and coach as inspirationally as they did. In summary, what my lecturers failed to do during my time on campus was to help me understand *why* I should read the books they recommended. They told me *what* to read ad nauseam (the recommended reading lists were stapled to the back of every handout, were pinned to every notice-board, and filled the final presentation slide of every class), but we were never told or shown *why* reading this book or the other would help us on our personal development journey.

My lectures started with the *what*.

My trainer colleagues at the beginning of my career, started with the *why*[1].

What, how, why. This explosively simple model comes to us from speaker and leadership expert Simon Sinek (2009). The golden circle, as he calls it, explains that to inspire and motivate we should start with the *why*, not with the *what* or *how* (Figure 2.1).

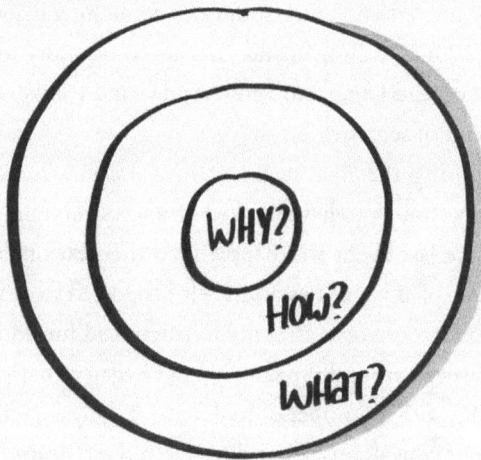

Figure 2.1 The golden circle

[1] Luckily, I have known the how (to read) since my mother taught me as a child.

Successful companies have long since known that starting with the *why* is the most powerful way to create saleable products and convince people to buy them. What companies like Apple(^{TM}) have become adept at doing is convincing us that having a particular tablet or gadget in our lives will ease communication, improve our efficiency, and generally better our experience. They explain to us why we need it in our world. They do not bombard us with how many gigabytes of RAM it may or may not have or how fast the CPU is. That is the *what,* and we can get to that. They start with the *why,* then lead us on to the *how* by showing us demos of happy customers swiping or pinching their tablet screens. The what is almost irrelevant to us, after that; just a bolted-on afterthought.

As a leader, *first,* explain to your team members why you are asking of them what you are asking of them or why you as a team are embarking on this course or setting up that project. Do not begin with the details of when the project meetings will be, what the project will be called, who will have which responsibility, and how the subteams are expected to communicate with each other. Start with the *why.* Help your associates to understand why they will be doing what they will be doing. When your team identifies with the why, they will develop better and better ways of how to accomplish the goals and the *what* will top all expectations. Your role as a leader is not to instruct intelligent, experienced, creative, out-of-the box thinking professionals on how to do their jobs, and it is certainly not to stubbornly remind them what they are producing or what service they are providing. Your role as a leader is to inspire them to appreciate what will be different when they have gone through those walls for you and the organization. Your role is to regularly and emotionally remind them of the why.

And remember, company values may differ from personal values (i.e. the why). Take the VW emissions scandal in recent years by way of an example. Mistakes were made, no doubt, and a culture of secrecy and deception seemed to have established itself in certain parts of the company. At least for a period. But, at the end of the day, decisions are made by people. The VW members of staff made certain decisions, some of which proved to be unethical and illegal, but these values probably differed from the company core principles. Decisions are made by people.

Decisions are not made by corporations. Those people-made decisions are swayed by personal values, and those values are the most delicate of leadership tools.

Leadership by Kitchen Table

Leadership is not a job. It is a mindset. There is no definitive list of characteristics that make up the perfect leader (Clifton, cited in Rath and Conchie 2008), and there are also no easy wins or quick fixes. Leadership is a constant reflection and reading of why a situation has developed and how to solve it. Irrespective of whether you are leading in business, industry, arts, armed forces, medicine, education, charity, civil service, religious institution, club or foundation or any other kind of organization, you will need to hone your leadership antennae.

My mentor and crackerjack Canadian leadership consultant Christiaan Lorenzen brilliantly slices the question of what makes a good leader down to a form that makes it comprehensible for any budding boss. When searching for the why and the how of leadership, all you need is to return to the kitchen table.

Leadership by kitchen table is, according to Lorenzen, the art of revisiting the communication basics we learned at our family's meal-time table. Think back to those gatherings. What fundamentals did we hear from our parents, guardians, or family? We picked up striking, focused, sticky messages of self-development, including (although the basics at each kitchen table no doubt vary somewhat) maybe the following:

Discipline: "Please be back in from play in time for dinner", my mother would say.

Self-management: My brothers and I had to wash our hands and look presentable at our dinner table.

Culture: The local rules of our table were learned from my parents, and subsequently taught by my brothers and me to visiting guests. At ours, these included passing dishes to those who could not reach and thanking whomever had prepared the meal.

Communication: "Tell us about your day, son." My father would invite, encouraging us to express ourselves communicatively, while also challenging us to actively listen to other discussions. "Listen to this story from your grandmother. You'll love this."

Transparency: If my brothers and I squabbled, our parents would encourage us to openly express our feelings toward each other and search for resolutions.

Delegation: The one who cooked needed not wash up. Also: "Would you serve, while I carve, please?" Dad delegated.

Strengths orientation: One cooked, one chopped, one laid the table, one played the piano to entertain after dinner, and everyone tried to tell the jokes (they were rarely funny!)

That is roughly what it looked like and sounded like in our dining room, growing up, and the fascinating thing is, and this is what Lorenzen is referring to, I have always lead my teams by the same principle values I learned at our kitchen table.

My communication is always transparent, active, and two-way, I delegate continuously, work hard to cultivate a culture of confidence and trust, I am diligent and self-disciplined, punctual, and honest, and I endeavor to manage strengths-oriented. I also like to tell (bad) jokes. But I get others to play the piano!

Our values in the workplace should be no different from what is important to us in our private lives. The way we treat people, the way we would like to be treated; I argue that there should be no difference at work. Some managers talk of being different at work. Why? The principles we learned at the kitchen table are those that guide us through our lives: basic fundamentals of respect, honesty, discipline, transparency, communication, and so on. Why should we not carry these values with us at the office?

For example, when two of your team members find themselves in a conflict, return to the kitchen table and reintroduce the essentials of transparency and honesty. Create an environment where both can candidly express their opinions.

If you feel that office rules are being bent, lunch breaks are getting longer, and personal matters or private distractions are detracting from the team's performance, return to the kitchen table and reinforce the importance of discipline and focus. Be a role model and show punctuality and discipline yourself and encourage others to follow suit.

When you find yourself in a sticky leadership situation at work and you are hard-pressed to find the right solution, return to your kitchen table. What value(s) would have been a foundation of your behavior then?

Identity

When I was 20, I was living on campus at university in London in the United Kingdom with five other guys renting an apartment. We shared cars to attend lectures, played sports together, had PlayStation marathons, and spent lots of the evenings partying and hanging out (*environment*). I was boisterous, loud, fun-loving, provocative, and hugely energetic. I also worked part time behind a bar to make a few bucks to pay for nights out (*behavior*). The only books I read were related to my studies, I knew a bit about the subject I was majoring in, but I knew a lot more about where the best karaoke nights and club nights were; I knew the pizza delivery number off by heart and my knowledge of premier league soccer was comprehensive. I was not very computer literate at that stage, but I was *au fait* with finding quotes from the right books in our extensive library to impress my professors in assignments (knowledge and skills). I loved the freedom of having recently left home for the first time and thought little about the future. I was invested in having a good time, learning, and making friends, and my attitude was to always try and get the most out of my time at the university (values, beliefs, and attitudes). I was a student. I saw myself as a free spirit, a friend, and the future of my country (role). I proudly wore my university's livery and colors at any opportunity, gave my all in the soccer team to beat competing colleges, and then sang traditional drinking songs with my fellow students to celebrate victory and taunt our defeated opponents. I would have laid down in traffic for my friends, but was single and did not have any children (affiliation).

20 years on and my life looks quite different. I have two children, I am married, and my wife and I own our own house in Germany with a yard for the kids to play in and a garage to park the seven-seater in (environment). I work and travel all over the world to different clients, and my wife and I spend our evenings enjoying a cup of tea on the deck, playing games with the kids or streaming new TV series (behavior). I have picked up a lot of knowledge about leadership, can recite most management models from

the literature of the last 50 years. I have learned and developed facilitation techniques and know the airport codes for most hubs in Europe. I have also become quite handy with woodwork tools, around the house (knowledge and skills). I believe that my hard work and strengths orientation will help my family and me enjoy a good life (values, beliefs, and attitudes), and my role today is that of a parent, husband, and breadwinner (role). Everything I do in my life is for my family and in particular to build a safe and loving environment for my children to grow up in (affiliation).

I am sure you will agree; that much has changed in my life in 20 years. It has changed for copious reasons (some planned and many accidental), but what is clear to me is that how I act and think today (my attitudes, behaviors, skills, and so on) has changed because my affiliation has changed. Affiliation, that is, your feeling of belonging, affects your attitudes, skills, behavior, and environment in an unstoppable cascade. Change your affiliation and your actions and drivers change. At university, my affiliation to the student life and to my alma mater inspired and influenced all my enterprise and wants. My current affiliation (my family) has driven a trickle-down change in everything I do and why I do it.

This model is adapted from Robert Dilt's Logical Levels model (Figure 2.2), which originates from neuro linguistic programming (Tosey

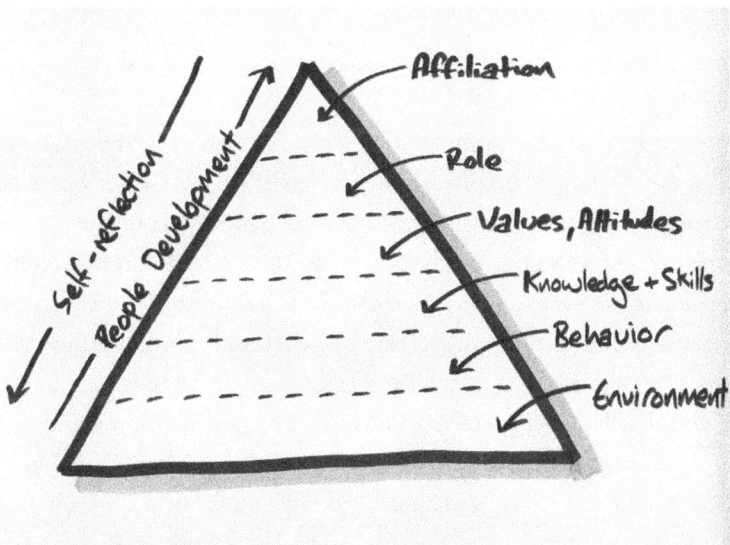

Figure 2.2 The logical levels of leadership

and Mathison 2003). Dilt's levels, often used in coaching, can function as an excellent self-reflection tool, but contemporaneously, also as a leadership mechanism.

We can use Dilt's model to ascertain which slice of somebody's experience they are currently focusing on. In doing so, we can help them better understand and self-reflect on their decisions and chances, and potentially, help develop them further. In order to sustainably affect behavior, it is vital to keep the person's values and beliefs in mind and to understand their role and to what they are affiliated. Leaders sometimes tend to approach a conflict or issue by attempting directly and pragmatically to solve the situation they see. Using the five levels from Dilt's, leaders can develop a better appreciation for why something is happening and fix it there, at the source.

Environment tells us about the where and when something is happening. It describes the setting and is important in establishing who is involved, where something happened and what the surroundings are.

Behavior tells us about what is going on and how people are acting. It is often what is noticed first about a person and is the side of people that others tend to talk to each other about. "He did this, she said that...." Behavior can be both verbal and nonverbal.

Knowledge and skills refer to a person's capabilities. What have they learned and how that is affecting their actions. It represents the how. In order to show behavior, someone has to draw down on a skill or on previously learned knowledge.

Values, belief, and attitudes often drive our behavior. The frustrating thing is that people are often not completely aware of what values and beliefs they hold. We may feel, instinctively and internally, that a particular course of action is right or wrong. This path of visceral; intuitive decisions can be traced back to our values, beliefs, and attitudes. They represent personal motivation and help us understand why someone acts as they do. Personal values may differ greatly from person to person and can be notoriously difficult to shake or adapt. We carry them with us always.

A role tells us who we are. We each have our own sense of self. Understanding our role helps us to appreciate why and for whom we are doing things. In this scenario, it does not refer to the role printed on your business card, but at a higher reflexive level; what are my responsibilities and on whom am I dependent and who is dependent on me.

Finally, taking its place at the very peak of the logical levels pyramid is affiliation. It can be difficult to put your finger on exactly what it is that you identify with, but according to Dilts, it drives everything else. All your beliefs, decisions, behavior, and so on. When we discover to what we are affiliated (i.e., a sense of belonging), it can be a very emotional experience and can be extremely powerful. To begin to understand your affiliation, ask yourself: Do I feel part of something greater than just me?

To grasp how affiliation cascades down to affect all the other levels, consider the assembly-line worker for the luxury car company, who will never be able to afford the product he makes and yet wears their branded clothes in his spare time, sports a tattoo of their logo on his forearm, spends what little money he has traveling to support their racing team, and collects miniature models of their cars. He identifies wholly with the brand, and this identity precipitates his role, behavior, and environment he establishes for himself.

Or, consider the young college undergrad, who despite having very little disposable income, spends all of her student loan to buy the latest laptop computer from Apple, which costs three times as much as a no-name notebook. A PC may suit her particular computer needs better, but she is determined to have a shiny Mac. she wants to be part of the gang. She already uses the smartphone and smartwatch made by the same company and all her friends have MacBooks. They are sleek, stylish, and totally cool. She identifies with the modern, dynamic image and believes that Apple have simplified the world with their intuitive devices, and that the Apple brand exudes class and modernity, yet she chooses to ignore the stories of poor working conditions for Apple subcontractor workers and the accusations of tax avoidance. Her environment, behavior, skills, values, and role have all been ultimately driven by her affiliation to the brand. Understanding to what your people feel affiliated can help you better understand their actions.

The model really comes into its own when we leaders are faced, together with our associates, with problems to solve. Apply the following two-step approach:

1. Identify at which level the problem is being caused.
2. To solve that problem, contemplate the situation from the perspective of a different logical level.

For example, if you witness unusually petulant behavior in one of your associates, assess their environment or their skills and knowledge. Might they be uncomfortable in the office in which they work or might they not possess the requisite skills to calmly perform their duties? If a team member lacks the knowledge in a particular field, coaching them on developing their admiration for the positives of training could affect their behavior. If a colleague is adamant that using very direct communication at all times is just and right, no matter how much others are offended, use the logical levels to better understand what his or her intrinsic beliefs and values are.

As Lowther (2013) puts it, "By shifting neurological levels, solutions to the problems become obvious." Understanding how the levels present themselves in your team and how they induce behavior can help you to coach them at times when they struggle with conflicts or are faced with challenges and so on.

Chapter Leadership Challenge

To be able to sell the why, we leaders first have to have bought into the why ourselves. Ask yourself at regular intervals why. Why are you at this organization and not at another? Is it for logistical or pragmatic reasons? Is your workplace close to your home or your children's day care? Or, is there another reason? When you applied for the position, what were the motivations for enquiring? Were you simply looking for something to pay the bills or was there another reason? When projects come down from your superiors, do you ask why the company is going in that direction? Can you see the *big picture*? Can you connect the dots?

CHAPTER 3

Let It Go

Some Leaders Take on too Much

In the Kingdom of the Blind...

There is an exercise we do with our workshop participants (I thank David Liebnau for introducing it to me), whereby everyone in the group is blindfolded. Two volunteers take on the task of leading the rest of the group, and their goal is to lead them to a certain meeting point (for example, a tree or a lamp post) a couple of hundred meters from the starting point. The leaders get to see the location of the goal and get to trace the steps there, but the rest of the team does not. The leaders explain the task, then don blindfolds themselves and the group, which often resembles a snake or a train of people, gingerly starts shuffling from the starting point. Most people are unsure when their sight is suddenly taken from them, and so take on a cautious approach and often self-protective body language and unusual walking style.

At some point, my colleagues and I remove the blindfold from *one* of the participants. That one person can now see. He or she has an ability or skill that by far tops that of anyone else in the team, and in turn, could take on the role of the leader, and yet, fascinatingly, more often than not, the participant who has their sight returned to them says nothing. He or she usually looks at us trainers despairingly, hoping for some sort of explanation, but they seldom tell the project leaders that they have a newly found skill set that could revolutionize how the task is completed.

At one such event recently, during the exercise debrief, the participant who had had her sight given to her, explained how she felt at that moment:

"I was unsure whether I was allowed to see or whether I was allowed to say anything, or not."

In other words, the unseen culture of *them and us*, that is, leaders and staff and each in their place was so powerful—even in a workshop game situation—that it restricted an intelligent professional from expressing her strengths. Interestingly, when asked if he would have relinquished control of the task to a member of his team, had he known that one of them could see (i.e., had skills to make the team more productive), the team leader stated that he would have immediately handed over the project lead to the sighted colleague.

After doing the exercise with another group recently, the first newly sighted team member said nothing. He shared with neither his leader nor his team mates that he could now see, and so could have helped the process and productivity. He stayed quiet. After a few minutes, I thus removed the blindfold from a second person. Interestingly, she also did not utter a word. She just continued as if she were blind, walking with her hand on the shoulder of the woman in front of her and with a hand from her follower on hers. I continued to free up the sight of a third, fourth, fifth, and sixth team member. At no time did any of them tell the leader that they could see.

Upon reflection, after the exercise, they shared with us their frustration during the task. They explained that they felt internally driven to say something, but all decided not too because they:

"Didn't want to ruin the game" or because they;
"Didn't want to hurt the boss's ego" or because they had looked around, could see that others could also see and were saying nothing and so assumed that;
"The culture of this team seems to be to say nothing, so I will also not say anything."

This is a classic example of the power of an existing culture to force others to conform and of the complicated (pseudo-political) dynamics at play in groups.

With an international group in a recent workshop, snaking its way to its goal on a Barcelona rooftop, the team leader (positioned at the front of the blind people-train) heard quiet discussions from the now-sighted team members, but sadly could not hear what they were talking about (they were discussing how they would use their sight to help the group and how they would communicate this to the leader). Assuming that the group could all still not see (he was none the wiser as he was blindfolded) and not knowing the true focus of the discussion, the leader screamed his dissatisfaction at the *lack of concentration, unfocused and irrelevant chit-chat*, and *disrupting elements* and ordered everyone to *shut up and listen!* There would only be one voice: his. The sighted members followed his order and said nothing, and the productivity of the group remained low.

Our responsibilities as professionals and leaders in similar team situations in the workplace are threefold:

1. We must develop a culture within our team, where ideas, suggestions, and proposals are respected and encouraged. We cannot afford to let our ego get the better of ourselves so much that it prevents us from taking advice and input from team members, who ultimately, could make the team more productive.
2. If we feel, as leaders, that there are team members who can improve productivity of or contribute positively to team goals, then we must hear them out. *My way or the highway* only reduces the number of creative minds at work to one. Be bold, encourage discussion, transparent opinion, and creativity.
3. If we find ourselves as the *newly sighted player* who has skills, knowledge, or creativity to offer, then we must find our voice. The knowledge is in the system (Baldwin and Linnea 2010). Not sharing that knowledge is the handbrake of innovation.

Let It Go

Talking of innovation handbrakes, the Peter Principle (Figure 3.1) is a theory posited by Laurence J. Peter in 1969 (Lazear 2000), which describes the all-too-common phenomenon of continuous promotion until failure kicks in. According to Peter, we have traditionally promoted those who are most successful in their role to take on a new role, and we do that until they have been boosted to a position to which they actually do not suit, and so fail, and are, inevitably, fired. Put another way, we all have talents

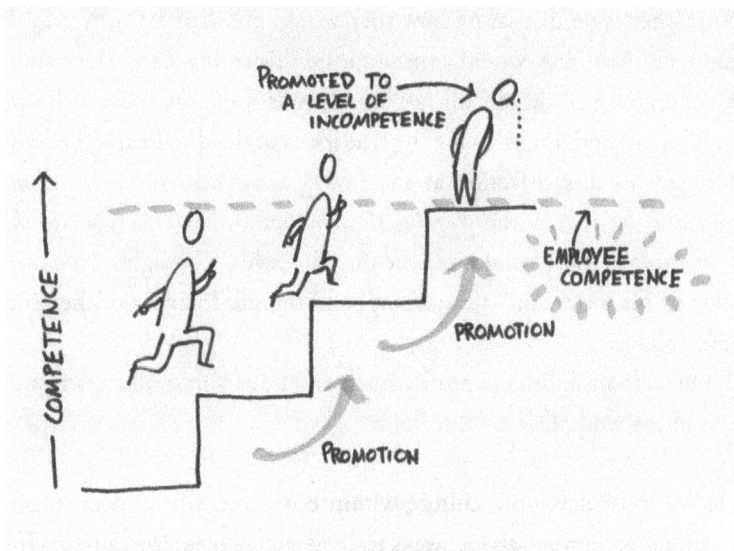

Figure 3.1 The Peter Principle: a good associate does not always make a good leader

and strengths (more on this in the next chapter), and it is the expression of these strengths that catch our superiors' eyes and sometimes lead to our promotion. However, it is very possible that we had the strengths in *that* role to catch the eye, but that by no means guarantees that we have the strengths to be successful in the *next* role. Just because I am the best in my field or the best in my team does not mean that I will necessarily be the best at *leading* that team.

The stage is often set as follows: the boss approaches, congratulates, and thanks for a job well done. She announces that the reward for your previous good work will be to head up the team that you were previously one of. In addition to that reward will be a car with slightly more horsepower, the word *manager* on your business card (which you will then quickly add to your professional social media page), a bit more money each month (after tax), no need to clock in any more, invitations once a quarter to team leader meetings, oh, and a heap of leadership responsibilities for which you have had no training and have no experience of how to deal with.

Put differently, you will be asked to do two jobs (will probably only be paid for 1.25 jobs), one of which you are totally inexperienced at and unqualified for. This enormous workload almost always leads to time management issues. The main bugbear of young leaders whom I coach is that they simply do not have enough hours in the day to keep all the balls in the air, and so they inevitably resort to type. To try to conserve energy, they focus on what they know, that is, the expert duties they previously did so well in, that it expedited promotion. They neglect the leadership aspects, so spending too little time with and too little time focusing on their team. This disconnect from the team, in many instances, leads to what I call *cocoon leadership*.

In cocoon leadership, the young leader, overwhelmed by the workload, ironically, makes life harder for herself by taking on *everything* that comes her way—good or bad. She retreats to her cocoon. Stressed and terribly fearful of failure (I could not possibly fail at my *first* job as a boss!), she convinces herself that undertaking everything and anything herself will be the best method of action. Of course, it is not. Our young leader has gotten herself into a vicious circle of over-responsibility. What she often fails to notice is that the sure-fire way out of this downward spiral is her team.

The more you lead, the less you have to *do*. By delegating tasks and responsibilities to team members, we not only free-up valuable time, which can then be directed toward other assignments, we (and this can be so efficacious) empower our staff to use their strengths to advance projects and solve problems. We kill three proverbial birds with one stone: we allow ourselves to develop, we help others to develop, *and* we get (people to get) things done!

Delegation, or as a popular song in a recent, family, animated film might call it; *letting it go* can be one of the most powerful devices in the leader's toolbox. You should not be scared to let it go.

The best way to let it go is to involve your team in decision making and task completion, that is, delegation. Mack Story (online 2018) adduces five levels of delegation:

1. *Wait until told.* Inexperienced leaders often keep their team waiting for things to do until they tell them. This, the lowest level of delegation, restricts growth, restricts respect, and restricts responsibility. In the short term, it can be effective, but in the medium and long

term, it squanders staff talents and escalates frustration and disengagement. Associates do not learn to think for themselves at this level, and the pressure on the leader is high, as he or she has to do everything himself or herself and stay mindful of what he or she has told the team.

2. *Ask what is next.* Worryingly similar to level 1. At this level of delegation, the only difference is that the team member returns to the leader to *ask* for their next job, instead of being *told*. Growth, respect, and development are also absent here, and the leader's time management is still challenged. The only difference is that the leader may incorrectly convince him/herself that the productivity is higher because his or her staff keep returning for their next mission.

3. *Recommend a course of action.* This is the level where the magic begins to happen. The leader has created an environment in which the associate feels respected, valued, and most importantly, *trusted* enough to approach, suggest ideas, and make recommendations. The leader no longer has the responsibility to determine the next steps. It has been transferred to the associate. If the leader disagrees with the suggestion, he or she can coach and ask questions to help inspire the delegate to new thought. If he or she agrees, he or she asks questions to understand and share the knowledge. A good leader will never take responsibility for any successes from the suggestion, though.

4. *Do it and report immediately.* Ownership starts to develop on the part of the associate at this stage. The suggestion bringer moves on from level 3, in that they need not first share the idea with the leader; they are trusted and empowered to complete the task without support. They need only report back on results. This completion before telling the boss feeds engagement and ownership, and the team member may begin to feel *part of something*. As we learned from Robert Dilts in the last chapter, this feeling of identity drives creativity and motivation. Unsurprisingly, the leader, at this level of delegation, is involved only a fraction of the time when compared with levels 1 and 2. Just think what you could achieve in that time!

5. *Own it and report routinely.* At this level, full responsibility and ownership has been transferred to the subordinate or team. The team simply reports their results to the leader at predefined intervals or

even when the leader or team member just feel the need. The person or team have the complete trust from their leader and this trust, in turn, frees both the team and the leader for other endeavors. As Steven Covey puts it (cited by Story 2017): "The beauty of trust is that it erases worry and frees you to get on with other matters."

Delegation not only eases pressure on oftentimes stressed managers, it breeds creativity, ownership, and trust, which, in turn, lead to motivation and increased team productivity. Give it a try. Let it go.

The Player-Coach

In professional soccer clubs in Europe, there is a sometimes personnel strategy whereby veteran players are promoted to the so-called position of *player-coach*. When a head coach leaves or is fired, a very small number of clubs have been known, on occasion, to ask one of their senior players to step up to the plate and coordinate team affairs (running practice, devising tactics, leading the team on game day, communicating with the press and senior franchise management, and so on), while *at the same time,* continuing as a player. In other words, these player-coaches are expected to look after their bodies, stay healthy, work on their technique, practice, and deliver high-quality performance on the field in as focused a way as they always did. However, unlike the rest of the roster, he or she runs practice himself or herself, and is not able to leave after practice. He or she remains at the training center and plans the next day's sessions with his or her coaches and formulates the team tactics to be used against the next opponents.

What is interesting about the player-coach is that he or she is very rare. In the highest soccer divisions in Europe, over the last couple of decades, there have been just a handful of player-coaches who have held their positions for anything more than just a small number of interim games.[1] Ruud Gullit (the Netherlands), Kenny Dalglish (Scotland), and Gianluca Vialli (Italy) are maybe the most successful examples of player-coaches. In U.S. sport, the phenomenon is even rarer. Tom Landry's appointment

---

[1] Thanks to Bert Smith Jr for his support with this chapter.

of Dan Reeves as player-assistant coach for the Dallas Cowboys in the NFL in the 1970s and Pete Rose's two-year stint as player-coach of the Cincinnati Reds in the MLB in the 1980s are two isolated examples of this uncommon appointment.

In professional sport, the player-coach is rare, and yet, it is very, very common in the corporate world. Almost every business in the world employs the strategy of promoting team members to leadership positions (see the Peter principle), but expects them to continue with their functional, technical and professional responsibilities at the same time. In a way, such corporate player-coaches are expected to do *two* jobs.

If you are reading this book, chances are you are already a player-coach or you soon will be. This transition from leading yourself to leading others *and* yourself requires a significant shift in mindset, and is maybe the hardest leadership metamorphosis there is. You need to learn to prioritize your tasks and hone your personal organization, while at the same time, developing skills, such as delegation, and communication with employees. Player-coaches have to move from trusting in themselves and their own abilities and strengths to extending that trust to others. Namely their teams.

Many young leaders struggle with this shift in paradigm and lots complain that they feel they lose control when taking on managerial responsibilities in addition to their process responsibilities. Young leaders oftentimes bemoan being forced to leave their comfort zone, and in particular, many note tension with having to delegate tasks, which they previously conducted competently themselves, to seemingly less-qualified colleagues. *Why should I give that task to him and watch him do it worse than I would, when I can do it fine myself?* I can appreciate why young leaders ask themselves this question. Before they were given added leadership responsibilities, they were good at their jobs. They were fast, efficient, skilled.

To try and detangle this conundrum, I would like to return to the player-coach scenario. Imagine you are a player-coach in a professional soccer team. You have chosen your team for the match and have included yourself in the on-field line up. It is the last minute of the game and the scores are level. Your team is awarded a penalty (similar to a field goal in football, in that your team could win the game with this one kick).

Who do you choose to take the penalty kick?

Maybe you are thinking:

1. "I am the head of this team. I will step up and shoulder the burden of such an important task."

   Or maybe:

2. "If one of my teammates shoots and misses, then maybe he/she won't be able to deal with the disappointment and it may negatively affect his future performance."

   Or maybe:

3. "I have the power to choose who gets the glory here, so I am going to take it myself and get the plaudits, if/when I score."

How about the following tactic?

Let the best penalty kicker in the team take the penalty.

In other words, divide your team's tasks up strengths-oriented. Who is the best at what? When you have identified your team's strengths, assign them tasks accordingly. That is leadership. Bearing the weight of a thousand problems yourself (see i) protecting your team from (potential) failure (ii) or taking the glory yourself (iii) (even if you are unsuited) is not leadership.

Leading is about getting the right people in the right place at the right time to deliver top performance for the team. To achieve that, you need to lead strengths-oriented.

Chapter Leadership Challenge

Check out *Delegation Poker*[2] by Jurgen Appelo.

Jurgen has designed a simple game that can be played by small groups with little effort (i.e., the playing cards can be downloaded for free or even scribbled on blank pieces of paper). The game even works as an individual, self-reflective exercise. Delegation Poker encourages players to reflect on the extent to which they would delegate responsibility in a series of short business cases. The players can then simply discuss their motivation

---

[2] https://management30.com/product/delegation-poker/

for delegating differently or discuss and keep score. According to Apello, there are seven levels of delegation:

Tell: the boss makes the decision and orders others to do it
Sell: the boss makes the decision and convinces others to do it
Consult: the boss asks for others opinions and then decides
Agree: the team decides together
Advise: the team decides, but can use the boss as an advisor
Inquire: the team decides and then the boss inquires after completion
Delegate: the team decides and implements alone

CHAPTER 4

Bee Glasses

Some Leaders Do Not Work Strengths-Oriented

The Jaggedness Principle

Just a few years after the war, the U.S. air force began to address an issue, which they had noticed had been steadily worsening for over two decades. Flying had always been a risky business, but with the advent of new jet technologies, safely controlling the ever-faster planes appeared to have become more and more challenging. The number of accidents had risen markedly, and most were blamed on human error as the aeronautic engineers insisted that mechanical failure was only at fault in the minority of cases.

Disgruntled pilots asserted that they should not burden all of the responsibility for the incidents, and so investigations were launched. All aspects of the flying experience were scrutinized, and in particular, the cockpit. It turned out that all pilot seat dimensions and their respective distance to pedals and other controls used by the U.S. Air Force had, since their design in 1926, remained the same. The assumption was made that the average pilot build might have changed in the last 20 odd years, and so data was collected to ascertain the 1950 pilot average body shape.

The hope behind the study was that, upon establishing the average foot size, waist girth, leg length, arm length, and myriad other pilot body dimensions, the engineers would be able to adjust the distance that the joysticks, controls, pedals, and so on find themselves from their pilots to optimize pilot competency, and so reduce accident statistics. In other words, the belief was that, if the cockpit is designed around the average pilot body shape, then the average pilot will be easily able to reach the controls, and so cause fewer accidents.

This assumption followed a popular scientific paradigm of the first half of the 20th century known as "typing" (Ogata 2001). Typing, its advocates claimed, was the science of drawing logical conclusions based on apparent data alignment. For example, if a group of thieves had been found to have had unusually large hands, then large hands might have been considered a strong indicator of criminal intent. If that had been the case, then goalkeepers, pianists, and basketball players with long fingers would, presumably, not have been trusted with one's valuables. But, by the same token, the assumption was that the average-sized pilot would make fewer mistakes if his or her plane controls were engineered in such a way that they were easily reachable.

So, in total, 4,063 pilots based in Ohio were rigorously measured. Then, using the body dimension data from the pilots, the Air Force designed a seat and cockpit that exactly fit the average U.S. pilot body shape. What do you think? How many of the 4,063 pilots represented exactly the body shape of this fictional *average U.S. pilot?*

Zero. Not one of them did.

Following the typing principle and falsely believing that the concept of average exists in humans and can be used to shape human surroundings, the U.S. Air Force ended up designing a seat that, while intended to fit everyone, indeed, fit no one. Not for the first time in the history of leadership and strategy had an assumption led to huge misunderstandings and the development of an ill-fitting strategy. The wrong environment was designed, based on the assumption that there is such a concept as the average person.

There is no such thing as average.

Certainly not with regards to developing an environment for humans to function in effectively. The people who work in your team are not average or even similar and should not be treated as such. Each human being is spectacularly unique, and I am not just talking about one person being taller than the other, and one having blue eyes and one brown. We have also evolved to be tremendously diverse with regards to our cognitive ability, and in particular, our personality. Social scientists call it the *jaggedness principle* (Rose 2017). Just as a knife's edge is jagged to allow it to slice through the bread, so too are we jagged in our difference from one another, in order to help us *slice* through the myriad and varied challenges of life on this planet.

As a leader, you have the challenge to tune your antenna to try to read and understand the people you surround yourself with. You should also enter into transparent discussion with your colleagues and invite them to share their opinions, values, and foci. You do not have to be their friend, but you have a professional responsibility to appreciate their difference, and not to consider them as typical or average, and so run the risk of making the mother of all leadership errors: treating them all the same.

Do You Want to Be a Bee?

Adding to our appreciation of colleagues as each being unique, let us turn our attention to our surroundings and how we interpret *them*.

Question: What do bees spend most of their waking hours doing?

They spend most of their time searching for pollen. And, where do the bees find most of the pollen? They find it in flowers and plants. Right? In other words, bees find what they are looking for in the beautiful things in the world. In order to achieve their goals, bees keep a lookout for and their antennae tuned in to what is great in the world. Bees recognize that, to produce more of their delicious product honey and to improve, to grow as a species, to be successful, they have to search for and highlight what is budding, prosperous, healthy, and successful in their environment.

Now, what do flies usually spend a lot of their time searching for?

That is right—shit!

Flies search for what is dirty; they search for where bacteria collects; they search for ugly, rotting, disappointing, decomposing, failed trash. Flies have developed a fantastic ability and super-fast reactions to enable them to find the ugliest things in the world.

My question to you is: Would you like to be a fly or would you like to be a bee?

Would you like to go through life only noticing mistakes and failure?, that is seeing the world through your fly glasses. Or, would you like to live with your eyes open and your antennae up, searching for and noticing what is good about what you see around you?, that is, bee glasses.

At a first glance, this might seem like a typically superficial self-help message: the type of calls to positive action that have become so popular on the Internet and social media memes, but I would sincerely like to invite you to read the next pages on the *bee mindset* (that is, *strengths orientation*) and *then* pass judgment. Strengths orientation and the bene-fits of positive psychology are not some hokum pseudoscience. They are grounded in decades of academic research (Seligman and Csikszentmi-halyi 2000; Seligman 1994, 1998, 1999) and have been shown to help productivity and increase performance (Asplund et al. 2016). So, let me share with you some concepts and research on strengths orientation effec-tiveness, and we will speak again at the end of this chapter. Okay?

Strengths Orientation

Let us go back to school!

What do you notice about the following picture (Figure 4.1)?

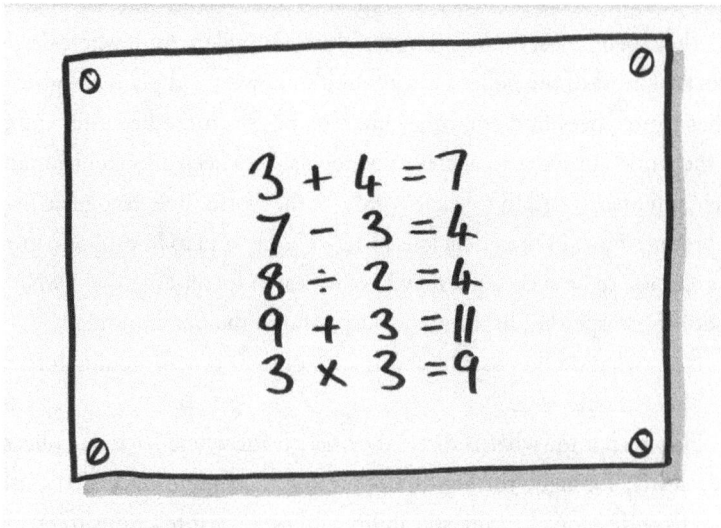

$$3 + 4 = 7$$
$$7 - 3 = 4$$
$$8 \div 2 = 4$$
$$9 + 3 = 11$$
$$3 \times 3 = 9$$

Figure 4.1 Math problem

Was the first thing that you noticed: the fact that one answer is wrong? The fourth equation is wrong. Did you notice the error first?

If so, okay. So, now, have another look (Figure 4.2). What *else* do you notice?

Five Are Right!

Five have been answered correctly, and yet, the vast majority of us notice first that one is wrong and neglect the fact that the positives in this

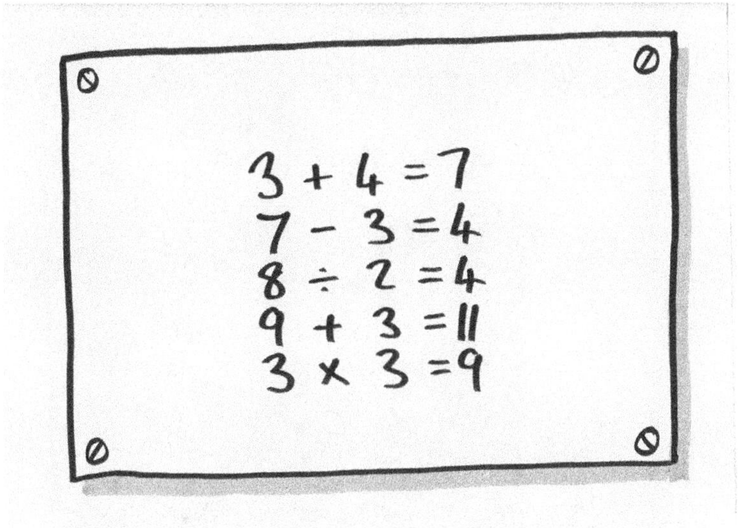

Figure 4.2 Math problem revisited

example far outweigh the negative. We have developed an ability in the western world to identify what is wrong with any given situation first (fly glasses?), often to the detriment of what is good. The Germans refer to this as finding *Die Haar in der Suppe* (the hair in the soup). Admittedly, a hair in your soup is not nice, but throwing the whole soup out or ignoring it or leaving it all to waste because of one discrepancy or investing all your energy complaining and addressing one small negative is not a high-performance attitude. What about a mindset of eliminating the weakness, but spending our time, energy, and money investing in developing what is already strong? What might happen if we invested in strengths?

Let us say that the math tasks we have just looked at were written by little Johnny. At the end of the semester, Johnny returns home with his report card and it looks something like the one shown in Figure 4.3.

When shown this report card, what would most parents probably focus on and assert their child to do? I predict that lots would spend time quizzing the child about the whys and hows of the poor math grade. Many would surely advise their child to work much harder in *that* subject in the future, maybe even if it means sacrificing other time-consuming pursuits to invest more time in math. *No more tennis practice until your math grade improves!*. Some would question or even chastise the teacher

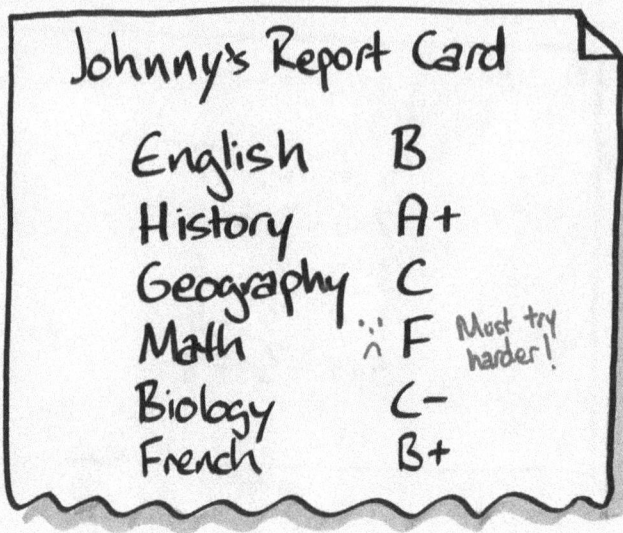

Figure 4.3 Johnny's report card

in a search for culpability. Some parents might find the time to support and coach their child with their math homework themselves, after school, and countless, no doubt, would pay hard-earned money for their child to attend extracurricular math tutoring, courses, or camps.

All of these approaches seem ostensibly meritorious, but they are squandering valuable energy, time, emotion, and in many cases, money. Assets that could be invested in developing strengths into excellence. Assuming that the reason for Johnny's modest grade in math is a lack of talent in the subject and not, for example, a poor relationship with his teacher or any other social barrier that hinders his performance in class, then no matter how much time, money, or energy we invest, Johnny will probably never become best in class in math. Think back to your school time and the subjects where you showed no obvious talent. Did extra classes or more determination lead to As?

I know that I was most certainly poor at math at school, and my mother and father dutifully spent hours helping me with my math home-work, often met with my teacher to better understand my errors, and they must have spent thousands of dollars over my time at high school, paying for extra math tuition that I hated going to every Wednesday for six long years. And, after all that time energy and money, how did I finish school? I scraped through with a *just passed* C minus in math. That is ok, I guess. But, I have spent the last decades reflecting on what might have come of me, had I spent even some of those Wednesday afternoons working on my talents instead of on my weaknesses.

Unquestionably, in most school systems that we have established across the world, failure in any subject, and in particular, in math is unacceptable. Many education systems expect at least a passing grade in math (and some other subjects) before the student can progress to the next grade or educational institution. Put another way, there is an *acceptable standard* expected of every student. In this case, math must be passed. Mine is not a critique of education systems here, nor of the need to be adequate at numerous subjects. If the school requires a certain acceptable standard in a particular subject, then so be it. If a company expects an associate to have abilities in several areas, so be it. As the student and his or her parents should work hard to achieve those goals, so must the modern employee be a jack of all trades. But, just passing or being a jack of all trades is not elite performance. Acceptable standard is not *best in class*.

If you want top performance, you have to develop strengths, not focus on weaknesses (Buckingham and Clifton 2001).

Now, with that statement, I am not proposing that you ignore deficiencies from now on. If you spot that the ceiling is about to fall in and injure a colleague, I am not suggesting you look the other way and let the plaster crash onto the acquaintance's head, mumbling, as you do, that you are employing a solely strengths-oriented approach. Acceptable standard, in this case, is that the ceiling remains safe and hung from the roof. Fix it. Have it fixed. Solve the problem. But, fixing the hole in the ceiling will not make it competition in terms of quality or beauty with the ceiling of the Sistine Chapel. Investing time, energy, and money into having the ceiling fixed will give you ... a fixed ceiling.

Fixing weaknesses leads to: fixed weaknesses. Nothing more.

If you want quality and best-in-class performance, you have to focus on strengths.

If a couple at home, wanted to get something down from a high shelf, the shorter partner would ask their taller spouse to reach up and get it. The taller person has a natural (physical) proclivity (height) that enables him or her to be able to reach high things. The shorter person could probably work around the situation with the help of a chair, stepladder, or by jumping, but all of those would exert unnecessary energy and time and probably not lead to perfect execution. If you want best-in-class, easy-to-implement performance with the minimum of energy wastage, get the person with the right talents doing what suits those talents. We seem palpably aware of people's physical abilities, but seem to have far greater difficulty identifying their mental talents.

The problem is that many of us have been working with certain assumptions (particularly in the business world) for a long while now.

Typical (False) Assumptions:

1. Anyone can achieve anything they want. They just need to want it hard enough and work hard enough at it. Anything can be learned.
2. People achieve success in the same way.
3. Eliminating failure leads to high performance.

Let us take a closer look at each of these assumptions, one by one. We have already seen that fixing errors does not lead to success, it just leads to fixed errors so that we can disregard assumption three, right off the bat.

What about assumption number one? We have heard this a million times, haven't we? It is what parents often tell their children, filled with parental pride. "You can achieve anything you want to, darling." "Follow your dreams. If you want it bad enough and work hard at it, you can become anything you would like!" "You would like to be a concert pianist, when you grow up? No problem. Keep going to music lessons and you'll play Carnegie Hall one day!" These statements and their intentions of support, love, and positivity are not what I am taking issue with here. I am, of course, an advocate for supportive, loving parenting and understand why parents tell their children such things. My issue is with the mindset that ensues after hearing such rhetoric again and again. It is the unrealistic mindset that anything can be learned, that anything can be achieved. Sadly, that is just not true. We all have different strengths and talents, and so, by definition, cannot all achieve anything we like. The tallest woman in the tribe is the only one who can reach the high-lying fruits (because she has a particular predisposition: height), and by the same token, the one with certain talents (predispositions) is the only one who can achieve greatness in any particular field. This is a fact of nature, and to be able to lead a high-performance team, we must accept that people have different talents, and that they cannot all achieve anything they want.

Let me give you an example. I was a good soccer player as a child. I represented my school through all age groups, played for a local club at the weekends, represented my district a couple of times, and there was talk that scouts from pro clubs were interested. The thing is, I wanted to become a pro soccer player so badly. It is all I thought about. I worked incredibly hard at it, too. I would practice at school in PE, then practice with the school team after school was out, then rush over to my club to train there, and then, come home and kick balls against the house wall (much to my parent's chagrin) until after the sun had gone down. I wanted it so badly. No one can accuse me of not trying hard enough, and I was quite good. But, (what I realize now is that) I did not have a natural talent; a predisposition for the technique required to be a top-class soccer player. I was told that I could read the game well (i.e., predict where the ball and the players would go), and this gave me an obvious advantage over my competitors. I knew every rule of the game and could use all the gray areas to my advantage over referees and opponents. However, I was a slower-than-average runner, not as agile as high-level soccer players, my ball control and technique was only okay, not great—despite hundreds of hours of practice—and my ability to convert the coach's tactics into plays on the field was patchy, at best, despite dedication and focus on my part. In summary, I had the knowledge and skills, but I did not have natural disposition (talent) (Figure 4.4).

Regarding the second assumption: one often hears from leaders: "I have had success leading by directive, so I expect you to manage your team with the same amount of command as I do." Or, "Sarah won the contract at the new client by creating lots of detailed reports for them so I look forward to seeing your analyses." We hear the assumption that people can achieve something that others have previously achieved and in the same way, but this is fundamentally untrue. People achieve success in different ways. Sarah clearly has a gift for compiling detailed statistical reports, but I cannot assume that her colleague will have the same analytical talent. The boss, in the preceding example, succeeded with transactional leadership

$$\begin{bmatrix} \text{SKILLS} \\ + \\ \text{KNOWLEDGE} \\ \times \\ \text{TALENT} \end{bmatrix} = \text{STRENGTHS}$$

Figure 4.4 Strengths are the combination of talent, skills, and knowledge

(see Chapter 8), but it is incorrect to assume that his protégé will not be able to lead his team productively with a more transformational (see Chapter 8) approach. You would not ask a quarterback to block. You probably would not expect the baseball player with the weakest arm to play at catcher behind first base, and you probably would not expect the drummer and guitarist in your favorite band to swap instruments for a big concert. Do not expect your team to all accomplish tasks in the same way, either. As the saying goes, "many roads lead to Rome."

We can develop new assumptions to work with a strengths-oriented mindset:

1. Some things can be learned, but most are impossible to master. There is a difference between skills, talent, and knowledge.
2. Everyone is on a different journey toward success. People get *there* in different ways and using different talents. There is no perfect way to achieve excellence.
3. Eliminating mistakes leads to eliminated mistakes (acceptable standard). To achieve best in class, we need to focus on existing strengths and talents with strengths-oriented leadership.

But, do not just take my word for it—take a look at some of the huge body of research that has emerged in the last few decades advocating a strengths-based approach.

Strengths Research

In a groundbreaking study, and the one that some argue began the strengths-orientation movement, Glock (1955) (Figure 4.5) found that greater personal development is possible when working with subjects who already have a natural talent for the pursuit. Glock took a group of students and looked at the speed at which they could read, and then had them train their reading skills in a series of speed-reading techniques. Before training began, reading speed was tested, and one group could read around 90 words per minute, while some showed an apparent disposition for speed reading and (without any learned skills) could read 350 words before the training started (group 2). After training, the first group showed, on average, an improvement in reading speed from around 90 words to 150 words per minute. So, the motto here could be: training works.

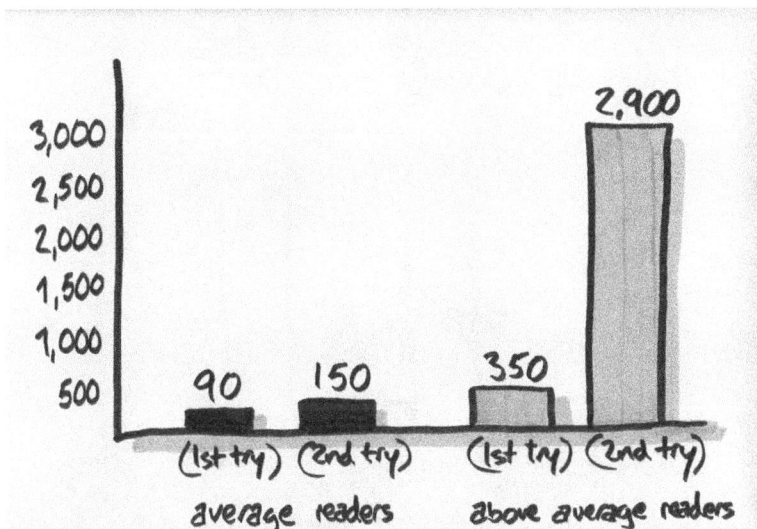

Figure 4.5 *The effects of talent-oriented training. Example: speed reading*

However, those who could read the fastest *before* the training was implemented (i.e., they showed a talent for reading quickly before they learned the skills and acquired the knowledge) could increase their reading speed in a marked degree from around 300 words per minute to 2,900 words per minute. The motto here is clearly: to get excellence, work with existing talent. Developing existing talents can lead to best-in-class high performance.

But, what about in management? How can a leader use the strengths-oriented approach to develop his or her team to be high performers? A large body of quantitative and qualitative academic and experiment-based research supports the effectiveness of strengths-based management. To mention all the studies that have shown positive managerial results from strengths-oriented leadership would, sadly, stretch the scope of this book, but here is a sample of such studies to whet your appetite and hopefully strengthen your interest in strengths-focused leadership.

One study (Figure 4.6) found that managers who focus on their associates' strengths are able to stimulate engagement in 99 percent of their employees (Gallup organization 2001), while another noted employees to be nearly 8 percent more productive in their role, when working in a strengths-developed environment (gallupstrengthscenter.com).

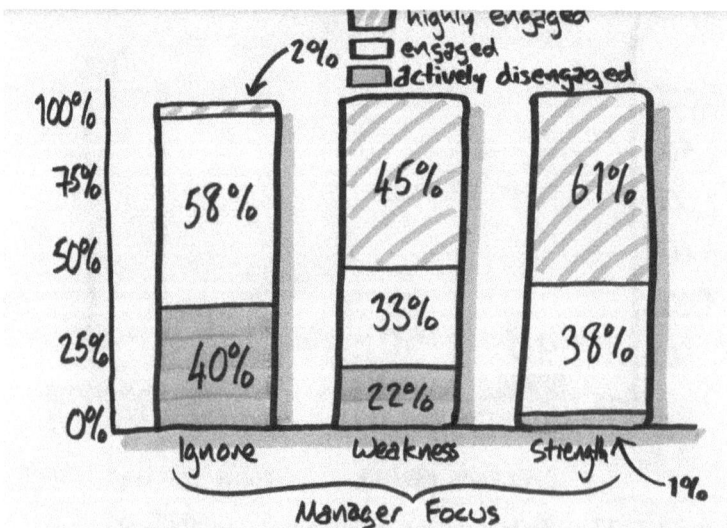

Figure 4.6 *Strengths-based leadership leads to employee engagement*

Another study of 2,000 leaders found that managers had an 86 percent chance (1.9 times greater than otherwise) of increased project success if they adopted a strengths-based approach to leadership, including matching task delegation to talents and prioritizing talent over seniority or experience (Gallup organization 2002). In a further study, workers who felt that they regularly had the opportunity to complete tasks in which they are gifted were found to be far more productive and exhibit a more competitive edge than those who do not (Luthans, Youssef, and Avolio 2007). Indeed, one study found that employees who benefited from strengths-oriented interventions are 44 percent more likely to score higher on customer relation appraisals and 38 percent more likely to show higher-than-average productivity than those who did not (Harter, Schmidt, and Hayes 2002; Harter and Schmidt 2002). A strengths-based approach to leadership leads to employee satisfaction, and numerous studies have shown that improved employee satisfaction leads to greater customer satisfaction (see Chapter 5). Using standard utility analysis techniques (Schmidt et al. 1979) to transpose these findings to quantitative profitability, it can be asserted that companies that embrace positive psychology and strengths orientation to leadership can generate over 1,000 U.S. dollars more productivity per employee (Schmidt and Rauschenberger 1986).

Most recently, in 2016, Asplund et al. conducted a huge meta-analysis of 43 studies investigating *the relationship between strengths-based development and business performance outcomes* (2016, p. 01). The study looked at 1.2 million people in 49,000 departments and teams from organizations in 45 countries. Asplund et al. (2016) note remarkable increases in customer engagement (between 3.4 and 6.9 percent), in employee engagement (9.0–15.0 percent), in profit (14.4–29.4 percent), and in sales (10.3–19.3 percent) and decreases in safety incidents (22.0–59.0 percent) in the business units explored in the research in which staff had the benefit of strengths-based interventions.

Focusing on associates' talents, assigning responsibilities according to their abilities, and embracing the philosophies of positive psychology in the workplace are not wishy-washy, the-glass-is-half-full, pseudo-science. It works. It helps managers and staff alike to be more productive (Albrecht et al. 2015; Buckingham and Coffman 2014). Indeed, "the relationship between strengths-based employee development and performance at the business/work unit level is substantial and generalizable across organizations" (Aspund et al. 2016).

I think that is enough science for a while. Suffice to say, the evidence is overwhelming: strengths-based leadership leads to increased productivity and higher performance across all sectors. Do you lead strengths-oriented?

Chapter Leadership Challenge

A well-established, powerful self-reflection and team-development exercise is the talent profile.

The scientists at Gallup, under the leadership of the godfather of strengths-based leadership, Donald Clifton, designed the Gallup Strengthsfinder™ (now named Cliftonstrengths™), an ingenious assessment tool grounded in and based on decades of research from interviews conducted with over two million employees, in over 190,000 work units, and at over 200 organizations (Clifton and Harter 2003). The assessment (by using 177 simple multiple-choice questions) "measures your natural patterns of thinking, feeling and behaving, so when you're done you'll have discovered your talents" (gallupstrengthscenter.com). The online test has been taken by nearly 18 million people,[1] including staff at over 90 percent of the Fortune 500 companies (gallupstrengthscenter.com), and if you find yourself with a spare 45 minutes or so, I strongly recommend you take the online test to receive feedback on which talents you are strongest in.

Reflecting on and creating your own strengths profile can be hugely rewarding and facilitate your task management and leadership. If you purchase a Gallup Strengthsfinder© (Gallup organization 2000) code, then base your profile on the top five strengths that the test spits out for you. If you choose not to take the test yet (and you can absolutely begin to reflect on your strengths without the algorithms), then simply use your own vocabulary and your own self-assessment of what you are good at.

Now, with your top five talents in hand, take a large piece of paper (working analog may seem old fashioned, but it fires up creative synapses that staring at displays and screens just does not muster) and create your talent profile similar to mine as shown in Figure 4.7.

---

[1] As of February 2018.

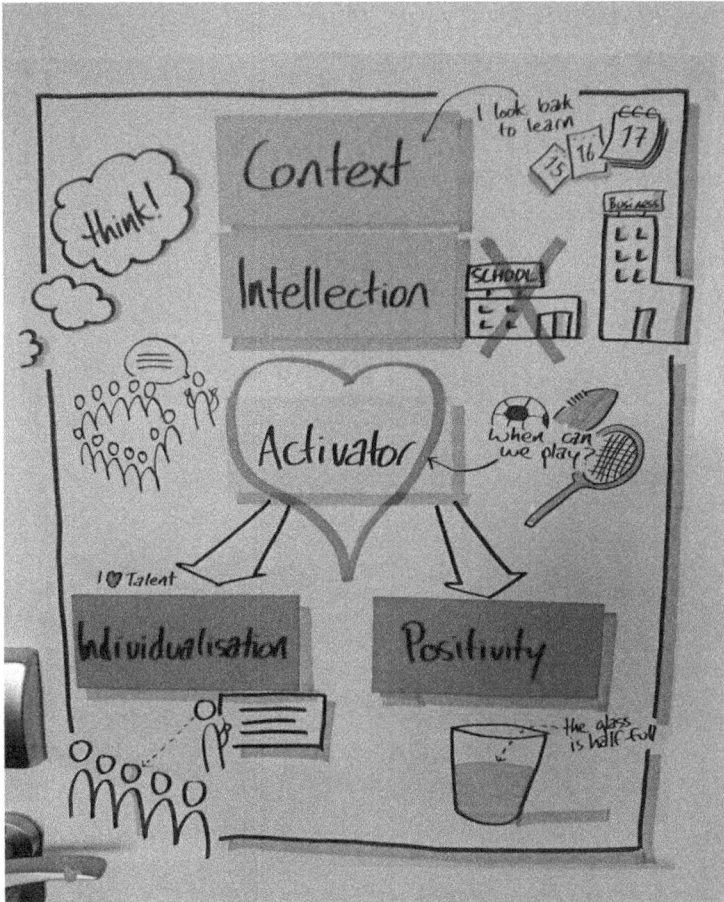

Figure 4.7 Top five talent profiles, Matt Beadle

Which way you organize your talents on the page and how you present them is, of course, entirely up to you. The exercise should serve as self-reflection and be honest and genuine. Gallup has found that people who have reflected on and identify with their talents are three times as likely to have superb quality of life and six times as likely to engage themselves in subjects and tasks that they do best (gallupstrengthscenter.com). Have a go.

After you have completed your profile, invite your team to create theirs and get together to discuss your combined strengths and how you can all apply them in the most effective way.

CHAPTER 5

Out with the Carrot and Stick

Leaders Often Make the Mistake of Only Motivating Extrinsically

The Status Quo

Does the basketball player, who gets paid 100,000 U.S. dollars per week score twice as many points as his team mate whose agent only negotiated their player a 50,000 U.S. dollar per week contract? Does the fat-cat CEO who sets himself up with a six million U.S. dollars annual salary plus bonus (paid out irrespective of whether or not targets are met) generate five million U.S. dollars more than a CEO paid one million U.S. dollars per year? (Ariely 2008). Do graphic designers create more innovative conceptions if they are threatened with redundancy if the next design is not groundbreaking?

Think of a task, that you do not enjoy doing. When you do this particular task, do you often watch the clock, counting the seconds until it is finished. It brings you no joy, and you do not consider that you are very good at it. Indeed, others (including your superior) have given you the feedback that you are not good at it. They watch over you closely to see whether or how badly you complete the task.

Would you perform this task better (i.e., deliver souped-up performance, resulting in improved overall quality), if I offered to paid you more than you usually get paid for it or threatened to fire you if you do not perform?

Many scientific teams over the years have looked at just these questions: Does more money motivate us to be more productive? Does fear of punishment drive us to better performance? In other words, does the proverbial *carrot* dangled in front of the *donkey* or the threat of the *stick* smacking down on its backside motivate the animal to deliver eminence?

The business world has predominantly worked on the premise of the carrot and stick since ... well since forever. Many companies (and this accelerated after the loosening of labor laws and employment restrictions in the 1980s) expect top performance, staff retention, and loyalty from their staff, but motivate solely extrinsically (Luthans 2011). Organizations sometimes offer only short-term contracts, fleeting periods of notice, or prolonged probation periods designed to drive hard work for fear of redundancy. Some offer benefits (for example, dental care) only after certain milestones have been achieved or after X years of service or set future pay-rises only when recorded achievements have been triggered. The fear of redundancy is very real for millions of employees (irrespective of whether this is voiced directly or implied more subtly), and huge numbers of people working today have success-related pay schemes built into their remuneration packages, whereby they have the potential to be paid more as long as they, their team, or the corporation achieves certain targets. Classic examples would be a salesperson, who, for every 1,000 gizmos he or she sells, earns 500 Euros more for the team, which, at the end of the fiscal year, upon reaching its targets[1] of units sold splits a (taxable) bonus pot.

This form of extrinsic motivation (i.e., motivation by tangible, outside factors) has created a high-pressure scenario in which we have been led to believe that, if we work harder, we will be paid more or at least not get fired. In many cases, such motivation does lead staff to toil and graft more, but evidence suggests that it does not bolster distinction. A paradigm exists where staff overexert themselves to achieve externally set goals in pursuance of their bonus payout. Meanwhile, many others work long hours to impress management, often clocking-up large accounts of (sometimes unpaid) overtime to avoid the dreaded sack and resulting unemployment.

For generations, an assumed staple of professional motivation, the carrot and the stick approach does not actually work. Extrinsic motivation sometimes makes people work more; it does not make them work *better*.

---

[1] Such targets are invariably established transactionally by management and are rarely determined autonomously by staff.

Despite overwhelming evidence to the contrary, generations of leaders, one after the other, have continued to tread the same path, and largely with the same unsatisfactory results. Try this[2]: make a fist with one hand. Close your fist as tightly as possible. Now, ask a friend to try to pry open your fist. Encourage them verbally as they do so, but keep your fist firmly closed the whole time. Let them try for a couple of minutes. They will almost certainly not be able to ease your fingers away from your hand; to do so would require a huge amount of strength and a much better purchase on your fingers. But, that is not the point. The point is that, your friend, nine times out of 10, will use the same technique for the whole two minutes. Most normally start by trying to get their fingers under your fingers to then pull them upward and outward. When this does not work, what do most people do? *More of the same*! Most continue (unsuccessfully) with exactly the same prying technique over and over again. Many people, when a strategy fails at the first attempt, employ exactly the same game plan again and again. It is time to break the mold, listen to what science is telling us about motivation, and rouse a culture of intrinsic motivation that spawns passionate high performance.

The Truth About Intrinsic Motivation

The science world has shown in copious studies that it disagrees with the business world's view that an offer of the carrot or threat of the stick expedites excellence. Extrinsic motivation does not lead to higher performance. It may, in some cases, lead to longer working hours and burnout (Lemyre et al. 2006; ten Brummelhuis et al. 2011; Bakker and Costa 2014), but it does *not* lead to better performance. And, at the end of the day, what is our goal as leaders if not to strive to develop our team and to aid them in getting the best out of themselves? In this section of the chapter, I would like to share with you the findings from a number of seminal studies, which vociferously suggest that leaders should be motivating in an entirely different way.

---

[2] Many thanks to Michael Knieling for this great little *aha* exercise.

Glucksberg, with two experiments (1962 and 1964), was one of the first in the modern era to investigate the correlation between extrinsic (in this case, financial) rewards and the quality and speed of completing conceptual, cognitive tasks. In other words, if I pay someone, then will they complete a task better than a person who has not been paid? Such positions are known as *if-then frameworks* (Winne and Hadwin 2008). In the study, Glucksberg asked two groups of participants to solve the cognitive performance test first designed by Karl Duncker in the 1930s and published posthumously known as Duncker's candle problem (Duncker and Lees 1945). The candle problem goes like this:

You observe some items on a table (Figure 5.1), near a wooden wall. Some tacks, a candle, and a set of matches. Your task is to firmly attach the candle to the wall, making sure the wax does not drip onto the table, using only the objects in front of you.

How might you solve this puzzle? You cannot pin the candle to the wall with the tacks; the tacks are too short; the candle is too thick. What is more, the candle wax breaks off when you stick a pin in it. So that is a no go. You can heat the candle with a match until it drips and then use the melted wax as adhesive to stick the candle to the wall, but you will find that the candle is too heavy for the wax to hold it.

Figure 5.1 The candle experiment

There is only one way to solve the conundrum, and most people stumble across it after a few minutes of consideration. Take the tacks out of the box, pin the box to the wall with the tacks, stand the candle in the box, and light it with a match. It seems so easy once you know the solution, right? But many of us do not quickly recognize the box as contributive. We appreciate the box only as a holder for the tacks, seldom as a distinct tool in itself. Or, indeed, some of us do not notice the box at all. This is called *functional fixedness* (Glucksberg and Weisberg 1966), that is, only seeing something in one state and not appreciating its potential other uses. Duncker's candle problem has been repeated by other scientists and with much larger sample groups, always with the same results (Adamson 1952).

Interestingly, if subjects are shown the tacks lying on the table outside of the now empty box, then the candle problem can be solved much more quickly. People almost immediately recognize the box as being helpful in the task and a potential holder for the candle, and there is little or no functional fixedness, so the task is easy. More on this later.

What Glucksberg found was that, if he incentivized people to solve the initial candle problem faster by pledging to pay the fastest 20 percent of people five U.S. dollars and the fastest of all 20 U.S. dollars (adjusted for inflation that's about around 40 and 160 U.S. dollars, respectively, today, not bad for a few minutes thought), then they, in fact, were *slower* than people who had not been paid or offered anything at all to decipher the same challenge. On an average, it took the group that was offered an extrinsic reward 3.5 minutes longer than those who were offered nothing. Glucksberg then restaged the experiment with one significant difference. This time he set the tacks up outside of the box and left the empty box in view on the table. This time around the incentivized group was faster than the other group.

So what does this all mean? It shows us that reward-based if-then signatures apply with straightforward tasks, but when assignments require more advanced cognitive processing, then promise of extrinsic reward can actually be counterproductive and produce *worse* performance. This seems to go against all we think we know about motivation. It seems to make little common sense, and yet, it is accurate. Dan Pink explains it best: "Rewards, by their very nature, narrow our focus. That's helpful when there's a clear path to a solution. They help us stare ahead and race faster. But 'if-then' motivators are terrible for [cognitive processing] challenges like the candle problem. (Pink 44) In fact Pink later goes further by adding that "'if-then' motivators that are the staple of most businesses often stifle, rather than stir, creative thinking" (46).

As this experiment shows, the rewards narrowed people's focus and blinkered the wide view. (Pink 44). It goes against decades of assumed logic, but extrinsic motivation does not improve high-level cognitive performance (i.e., exactly what we expect from our teams every day). But, one swallow does not make a summer. That constitutes just the result from one guy's experiments. What do other scholars have to say about motivation?

One could argue that the reward amounts in Glucksberg's study were too small to strongly affect subjects' motivations or levels of effort, but similar experiments have returned comparable results. In the United States, five U.S. dollars is a small amount of money, but in some countries, it carries far greater value due to different economies and buying power.

A group of U.S.-based academics (Ariely et al. 2009) investigated the effect of extrinsic motivation, in a similar study to Glucksberg (1962, 1964), but took their study to Madurai, India. With the price of living and earnings-to-value ratio markedly different in India, significant rewards could be offered without blowing the academics' budget. They got a group of participants to complete a series of tasks that tested their motor skills, concentration levels, and creativity. The subjects were split into three groups, and all were set certain targets in each of the exercises. About 33 percent of the group was told that they would be remunerated with a small monetary reward (4 rupees: around 50¢ or equivalent to about one day's pay) if they reached their performance targets, another third would receive a medium-sized reward (around five U.S. dollars, equivalent to about two week's pay), and the last group was promised a very large reward (about 50 U.S. dollars: around five month's pay) if they met their targets. The results, again, contradicted popular motivation wisdom. The group paid the largest extrinsic rewards fared the worst in eight out of the nine exercises.

In yet another study, The London School of Economics (2009) looked at over 50 financially incentivized payment schemes and found that, rather than motivate positive behavior, pay-for-performance plans actually stymie effectiveness.

> We find that financial incentives may indeed reduce intrinsic motivation and diminish ethical or other reasons for complying with workplace social norms such as fairness. As a consequence, the provision of incentives can result in a negative impact on overall performance (Irlenbusch cited in Morningstar 2012, p. 7).

Leaders commonly reward KPI-derived and measurable performance, and not creativity. Consequently, employees often offer up this type of more-of-the-same performance rather than creative thinking (Eisenhower and Shanock 2003). As we have seen, motivation narrows focus, and this narrowing—often caused by blinkered attempts to achieve goals—in addition to stunting creativity and excellence can also precipitate unethical, untrustworthy behavior, risk-taking, and decreased cooperation. The staff sees only the goal and may employ any means to justify the end.

Looking into the effects of motivation on creativity, Harvard academic Theresa Amabile (1996) set up a clever study where she had 23 artists present 20 paintings each to a panel of art experts. Half were commissioned and half noncommissioned. The panel judged the commissioned paintings (i.e., those that were ordered for payment) as "significantly less creative" (Amabile, cited in Pink 45) than the ones that were simply created for the artist's own pleasure. What is more, the artists noted their lack of joy and the creative restraint that they felt when producing work on demand.

This is known as the Sawyer effect (Ariely, Loewenstein, and Prelec 2006): Mark Twain's famous hero Tom Sawyer, once lumbered with the chore of whitewashing a huge fence in the mid-day sun had the brainwave of persuading his friends to take over his work by convincing them that it was a rare opportunity to be able to do such a task (scarcity, see Chapter 9), and that many had previously wanted to (consensus, see Chapter 9). As he sat on a nearby tree stump watching his peers gladly complete the task, which he had only minutes before hated, he mused that "Work consists of whatever a body is obliged to do, and that Play consists of whatever a body is not obliged to do." If we present something as work by offering a reward, then people we are trying to motivate instinctively recognize it as undesirable. The potential issue here for leaders is that we also set a precedent. If I ask you to complete a task that you do not want to do and you say no, maybe I could offer to reward you for it. The thing is, I will now have to reward you every time in the future, to the same level, to bag your compliance.

We have looked at the carrot, but what about the stick. Surely threat of punishment compels people to follow rules. Doesn't it? Gneezy and Rustichini (2000) observed a daycare facility post a sign to warn delinquent parents that if they turned up late to pick up their child they would in future be faced with a fine. After the notice was posted twice, as many parents on average as before arrived late to collect their sons and daughters. The threat of the fine, hoping to hone parents' feeling of responsibility, and prime their behavior, served the opposite and encouraged unpunctuality. The fine, instead of motivating good attitude, had turned a human relationship between the parents and teachers into a transaction. Now, the parents could simply buy extra time, if they need it (Suvorov 2003).

The carrot and the stick do not work. To stimulate cognition, creativity, and desire, people require intrinsic motivation. Dan Pink cutely sums up the dangerous side-effects of extrinsic motivation in his seven deadly carrot and stick flaws:

1. They can extinguish intrinsic motivation.
2. They can diminish performance.
3. They can crush creativity.
4. They can crowd-out good behavior.
5. They can encourage cheating, shortcuts, and unethical behavior.
6. They can become addictive.
7. They can foster short-term thinking.

Now, I would like to make something clear at this point. I am not saying: money is not nice. It helps us fund our lives and keep our family safe and warm, and that is doubtless a good thing. I am not saying: we should stop remunerating our staff. I am not saying: people do not work for money and enjoy earning, having, and spending money. What I am saying is that, after a certain socially acceptable level of remuneration that is comparable in that industry, people are content in their roles. To encourage best-in-class performance, out-of-the-box thinking, and state-of the-art creativity, leaders need to plug in intrinsic motivation for their teams.

High-Performance Motivation

If we cannot coerce preeminence out of our teams with the proverbial carrot dangle or with the intimidation of the stick slap, how can we get our guys to perform?

Luckily, many experts have looked at the subject of extrinsic motivation, and some have proposed starting blocks to help employees discover their own intrinsic drivers. At the first reflective stage, intrinsic motivators can be divided into 12 categories (see the following table). This list of drivers should by no means be construed as conclusive, but as a helpful suggestion of the types of areas one should look at to glean intrinsic motivation. This list has been compiled from eight models on human needs and desires.[3]

Table 5.1 Common intrinsic and extrinsic motivators

Responsibility Loyalty, integrity, principles, values	Autonomy Freedom, independence	Curiosity Learning something new, collecting experience, wanting to understand, thirst for knowledge	Social Recognition Social acceptance, affiliation, recognition in social networks
Well-being Relaxation, emotional security, without stress and fear, inner peace, calmness	Ownership and Wealth Accumulation of material goods, property, assets, wealth	Performance and Competence Leadership, influence, ambition, success, effectiveness of one's own actions	Fairness Social justice, social involvement, compassion
Collegiality and Care Friendship, meeting, social contacts, proximity, helping	Status *Social standing*, title, privileges, exclusiveness, prestige	Challenge Competition, rivalry	Structure and Security Stability, clarity, good organization, structure, detail

---

[3] Hierarchy of Needs: Maslow (1971); ERG Theory: Alderfer (1969); System of Needs: Murray (1938); Life Motives: Reiss (2004); Theory of Motivation (Kasser and Ryan 1993), Self-Determination Theory: Ryan and Deci (2000); Needs Theory: McClelland (1951).

I make that 48 drivers that scientists suggest may intrinsically motivate people to work better. The problem with this list, as I see it, is twofold:

1. Most of your team, when shown this list, will probably highlight different selections from the table as their own personal drivers. Helping each member of your group identify their own motivators may prove fiddly.
2. Your leadership would have to be so situational (see Chapter 8) as to be microscopic in order to constantly seek to motivate all at their own, individual level.

Thankfully, Pink (2010) has provided us with a much simpler, concise model of intrinsic motivation that is both easy to recognize for the employee and manageable for a leader. According to Pink, we, as leaders, have a responsibility to create an environment where our subordinates, with our support, can blossom in a climate of trust and be purely and intrinsically motivated by giving them just three motivational foci: autonomy, mastery, and purpose.

Autonomy

Let your people work when and how they want to. When leading your team, instill the *why* in them (see Chapter 2), but leave the *how* up to them. Entrepreneur and multiple company CEO Jeff Gunther calls this ROWE: results-only work environment (Forbes online). In ROWEs, it is irrelevant when people show up for work, where they work, and with whom they collaborate. It is only important that they deliver results. Give talented people the tools they need, but also, critically, the space they crave to work autonomously, and they will be driven to achieve for achievements sake. No carrot in sight. Teleworking, flextime, and spatial decentralization have all been shown to positively affect industrial performance (Martínez Sánchez et al. 2007). If your company regulations allow (see Chapter 11), then let your team off the leash, transactionally set goals together with them (see Chapter 8) and let them work as autonomously as possible.

Mastery

Have people doing the things they are great at. There will be lots of overlap on this point with Chapter 8, so please check that out too, but, in short, people achieve best when they are doing what they love. When we work autonomously, we are engaged and driven to want to improve. Sadly, this engagement is lacking in so many modern offices and workplaces. According to a McKinsey study, in some countries, no more than a few percent of the workforce claims to be engaged in their work all the time (Kirkland 2009). But, outside of the workplace, it proliferates. Mastering a challenging skill, be it painting that landscape, climbing that rock face, or building that tree-house, we would all do any of these and more stimulating, fascinating, challenging tasks for no money, just for the thrill of being able to say afterward: "I did that." Millions of us take dance classes or learn musical instruments or uncover the artistry behind creative writing or sculpture, or whatever. We do all these things for free. Amateur musicians spend hours practicing their scales because it makes them better, and that development of mastery is powerfully addictive. In such pursuits, the activity is reward in itself. Motivation and happiness guru Csikszentmihalyi (1997) called these *autotelic* experiences (from the Greek for self (auto) and the Greek for goal (telos)). He later shortened the word to the far pithier: flow. One simple question: why don't your people deserve as much autotelic experience at work as they have in their private lives? Just think what they might achieve if they were in flow every day.

Purpose

If you were to draw a graph with time (let us say the last 100 years) on the x-axis and numbers of engaged workers and numbers of people volunteering for good causes on the y-axis, you would see the engagement line steadily heading down, but being intersected by the volunteerism line rising exponentially. In the last couple of generations, the numbers of people searching for a purpose in charities, clubs, schools, political parties, good causes, social or environmental groups, and so on has continued to rise, while worker engagement falls year on year. This suggests that people are searching for something in their voluntary contributions that they are simply not finding at work. What can we learn from this social activity?

A survey commissioned in the United Kingdom in 2015 found that 58 percent of full-time staff (and 70 percent of part-time staff) feel that they have little or no influence at work, and 59 percent think they have no control over big business (UK.coop). Many seem disillusioned with the business world they work in and feel their contribution changes little. Many recognize little purpose in their work.

Such industrial disenchantment is one of the main reasons why we have seen such a dramatic rise in cooperative-styled startups in recent years (uk.coop). A cooperative (coop) can take many forms, but recently, we have seen numerous not-for-profit or profit-sharing organizations, that is worker cooperatives managed or owned by the staff, and consumer cooperatives that are managed by their customers, popping up. What is most intriguing is not so much that many seem drawn to businesses operating under a cooperative framework (as employees and as customers), but that such organizations are so successful. A 2007 study found that 90 percent of the coops were still operating after five years, compared with 3 to 5 percent of traditional corporations. The 30,000 cooperative companies in the United States in 2009 helped create over two million jobs and contributed over 150 million U.S. dollars to the U.S. economy. People seem to want coops to work. Coop members share a vision that drives them to not let them fail (http://geo.coop/story/fact-sheet).

Now, I am not proposing you all quit your jobs and go set up coops tomorrow. That is not the message here. The coop, like any other company form, has its pros and cons. Of interest here is the drive, connection, and motivation that is often shown by coop members. They identify a purpose in their work; they recognize direction; and they are prepared to invest significant time and energy (irrespective of material gains) to contribute to that shared success. We can certainly learn something for our capitalist companies about the power of purpose as a motivator from such constructs.

Chapter Leadership Challenge

What motivates you, and how would you like to motivate? Go back to the motivators in Table 5.1 and develop a personal ranking for you. Which of those would motivate you the most to bring best performance, and which would you need the least? Reflect and make notes on *why* each motivates you.

Next, think about your team or, if you do not yet lead a team, your process partners or colleagues. What do you think motivates them? Again, make a list and then transparently discuss your thoughts with them. The more we all know about what motivates each other, the more focused and happy we can all work.

CHAPTER 6

The Rush Hour of My Life

Leaders Underestimate the Real Danger of Work Overload

Stress

I commute back to Italy, from Germany (where I work), once per week. I stay in an apartment during the week and fly home to see my daughter and my wife on Friday nights. I then leave for the airport to return back to work, on Sunday afternoon. My daughter is fine with it. When she was small, I used to commute to Paris. She's never known any other way of life, so that's fine.

—Paolo, Italy

I haven't seen my children except for weekends, for months. When I leave for work, they are asleep and when I return home it is too late to wake them. Even worse, I haven't talked to them about why Daddy is never there. I want to do that but I haven't got the time at the moment.

—Vasily, Russia

I mainly only see my husband, these days, over [video call].

—Stefanie, Germany

It wasn't until I suffered my heart attack and then, shortly afterwards, my wife was diagnosed with cancer, that I realized that I had got this work-life-balance thing all wrong. I would strongly advise younger managers to delegate more, in order to free up more time and space.

—Craig, United Kingdom

In Japan, it was common for us to stay late. It was rare for me to leave the office before 10pm or 11pm, sometimes midnight. Then the company insisted we go home at 9pm. Nothing changed so now they turn off the air conditioning at 9pm. It's still as it was, though. People now just work in the heat and humidity for a couple of hours.

—Takeshi, Japan

I'm 35. I work very, very hard but that's ok because I'm in the 'rush-hour' of my life. From 30 to 50 it's fine to work really hard. I'll slow down a bit, when I'm in my 50s.

—Tomas, Sweden

These are some quotes from coachees of mine on the subject of time management. All the speakers are aged between 26 and 50 years, and all are leaders. Some, like Takeshi who has 45 direct reports, have large numbers of staff to manage, and some, like Stefanie who heads up a three-person team, have responsibility for fewer, but they (and many, many, many more leader-executives like them, whom I train and coach) all have one thing in common: They have enormous workloads with constituent strains on their schedules and work-life balance.

Driving the leadership bus does not only entail the day-to-day steering of the vehicle. Imagine, as a bus driver that you would be required to consider the personal development, strengths and weaknesses, communication and organizational skills, personal problems, promotion opportunities, and conflicts of all the passengers on your bus—even after you and they had alighted and gone to your respective homes. As we have discussed in previous chapters, leadership carries with it great responsibilities, most significantly, responsibility for humans, and often, their dependents. This extra burden—the paradigm shift from leading myself to leading others—can take its toll and be very demanding both emotionally and chronologically. The leader does not just *park the bus* at the end of the day, leave her seat, and toddle off home to her hobbies and pastimes. Leaders do not have the luxury of leaving their work on their desk, when they leave for home. Leadership can be a way of life; not just a job.

Most leaders report both an increased operative workload (due to greater amounts of meeting invites, human resources issues, workers council matters, report reads, presentation briefs, and so on) combined with additional cognitive and emotional pressure stemming from strategic responsibilities, reflection on team dynamic, staff strengths and weaknesses, conflicts, communication breakdowns, personnel challenges, and the like. If it were only the former (increased operative tasks), many would, no doubt, be able to assimilate better, but it is the latter (the stress of and reflection on managing teams and their idiosyncrasies) that encumbers young leaders most. Balancing work and private life commitments and being aware of and nurturing energy levels are two prevailing stress tests of the young leader.

I know what some of you might be saying (and I also very often hear such pretension from my participants): "I'll be ok… I'm stressed now, yeah, but I'll get through it… I'm young and healthy, I can cope with it…. I'll slow down later…. I am under pressure but I have no option the bills need to be paid… Heart attacks are for old people… I'll be ok."

You may be okay. I sincerely hope that you are okay, but it is a truism that work-related stress is a very real, present, and worsening issue. A recent study found that 73 percent of the respondent working adults aged between 20 and 64 years reported suffering from stress, and that work is the most common cause of that stress (Statcan). What is more, our stress levels are rubbing off onto others, as noted by the American Psychological Association. "While 69 percent of parents say their stress has only a slight or no impact on their children, just 14 percent of youth say their parents' stress doesn't bother them (APA.org)."

Furthermore, the headache (pun intended) with all of this is that stress has a very real and physiological reaction on our minds and bodies. Chronic stress can lead to sleep disorders, back pain, headaches, panic attacks, burnout, tinnitus, and other afflictions (Techniker Krankenkasse 2012). An employee at a global player recently told me that the average age of death of their senior managers (64–67 years) is nearly two decades under the western world average. In fact, the Japanese have developed such a culture of overwork in recent generations that they have had to coin a term to describe what can only be translated as *death by overwork*. They call is Karoshi (過労死) (Nishiyama and Johnson 1997). South Korea and China evidently have a similar need for the term calling the gruesome phenomenon gwarosa (과로사/過勞死) (FT.com, Park 2016) and guolaosi (过劳死) (Oster, Bloomberg 2014), respectively, in their languages. I urge you not to make the mistake of thinking that such a dark wave will never affect western workers' as much as it does in Asia. Prevalence of work-induced stress is on the up—44 percent of the people claim that their stress levels have risen in the last five years (APA.org)—and left unchecked, stress can develop into a very real and serious problem (Aldwin et al. 2017).

The classic metaphor for this is the frog in hot water. If you drop a poor frog into a pot and then slowly up the water temperature, the animal will continually adjust itself to the increasing heat; its stress receptors not correctly recognizing and identifying the calefaction. It will struggle through the last phase as things get unbearable, but it will sadly die when the water gets too hot. If, however, you were to drop a frog into an already boiling pot of water, it would immediately sense the extreme nature of the situation and jump from the pot to safety. Stress can creep up on us. We adjust well to increased stress and our brains develop coping mechanisms, which allow us to soldier on and borrow energy stores from other bodily systems (Fabritius and Hagemann 2017); yet, they can, in fact, hinder us in the long term. When we cope with stress, we do nothing more than hide it away. We do not solve the problem. The water gets hotter, but we stressed frogs do not leave the pot.

Such chronic, slow-burn stress can be easily understood as a chain (adapted from Kaluza 2018).

Stressor–attitude–reaction (adapted from Kaluza 2018).

In the stress chain, something or someone stresses us. This is a *stressor*. The impact is from the outside: external. Workload, time pressure, disturbances, conflicts, demands from others (and more) are commonplace stressors. The stressor seems unavoidable and causes us to work, think, or act differently, and this fuels the next link in the chain: *attitude*. How we emotionally and cognitively deal with stress, combined with how we put ourselves under pressure, can strikingly affect our stress levels.

Be perfect: a striving for perfectionism, often expressed as impatience.
Be strong: the lone warrior syndrome (wanting to solve everything on your own).
Be loved: a desire to be recognized or admired.
Be careful: a desire to be careful.
I cannot cope: fear of failure and deficient self-belief (Kaluza 2018).

These are the five prototypical attitudes found in overworked professionals, and all stoke our stress fires. The final, potentially destructive, link in the stress chain is our physiological, emotional, cognitive and behavioral kickback to the damage inflicted by the *stressor(s)* and our *attitude(s)*. This is known as *reaction*.

Reactions to stress differ greatly from sufferer to sufferer, but they can include, but are not limited to:

- Warning signs of physical reactions: heart palpitations or abnormalities, breathing problems, sleep disorder,[1] chronic tiredness, muscular tension, digestive problems, headaches, back pain, loss of appetite, sexual dysfunction (Kaluza 2018).
- Warning signs of cognitive reactions: constant cyclical thought, concentration disturbance, nightmares, day mares (picturing negative scenarios), drawing a blank. Warning signs of emotional reactions: nervousness, inner restlessness, feelings of fear, dissatisfaction, apathy, sexual listlessness.
- Warning signs for cognitive reactions: aggression, impatient fidgeting, irregular alcohol or caffeine or tobacco or food consumption, interrupting people, ignoring others, stuttering or garbling words.

When we notice the warning signs, if we act quickly, we can control our stress levels and so dampen the effect they have on body and soul.

Dealing with Stress

Kaluza (2018) suggests three approaches for managing the three links in the stress chain, one for each.

Instrumental Stress Competence

To endeavor to reduce the magnitude of external stressors, and in doing so, reduce the adverse effect the stressors exert on you, explore methods

---

[1] Barnes, Lucianetti, Bhave, and Christian. (2015) found that leaders who slept less than average, or reported poor quality of sleep, were far more likely to act aggressively or discipline unfairly at work.

to improve your self-organization. Sadly, many external stressors cannot be avoided completely but many can be tapered with instrumental stress management. The classic instrumental stress management tool is the simple to-do list. However, one suggestion to implement before the to-do list, to aid time management and reduce stress, is the task-relevance portfolio.

Take a pen and a piece of paper.[2] We are going to work analog for a few minutes. Draw a table (Figure 6.1) and label the four columns as per the picture:

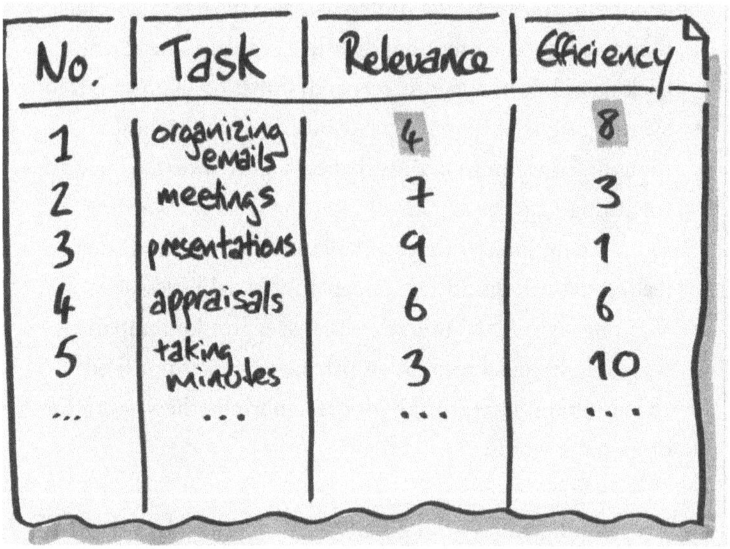

No.	Task	Relevance	Efficiency
1	organizing emails	4	8
2	meetings	7	3
3	presentations	9	1
4	appraisals	6	6
5	taking minutes	3	10
...	...	...	...

Figure 6.1 The task-relevance portfolio: reflection

In column 2, list 10 to 15 typical tasks that you regularly (have to) take on in your daily work routine. Number them 1 through n in the first column. In the third and fourth columns, subjectively score from 1 to 10 (1 is not at all, 10 is very much) each task for its relevance (column 3) and as to how effectively you implement it (column 4). For example, in the following table, the manager deems spending time to organize e-mails as not very relevant (4), but feels that he or she is quite efficient at it (8).

---

[2] I am grateful to my colleagues at the SYNK Group for this exercise.

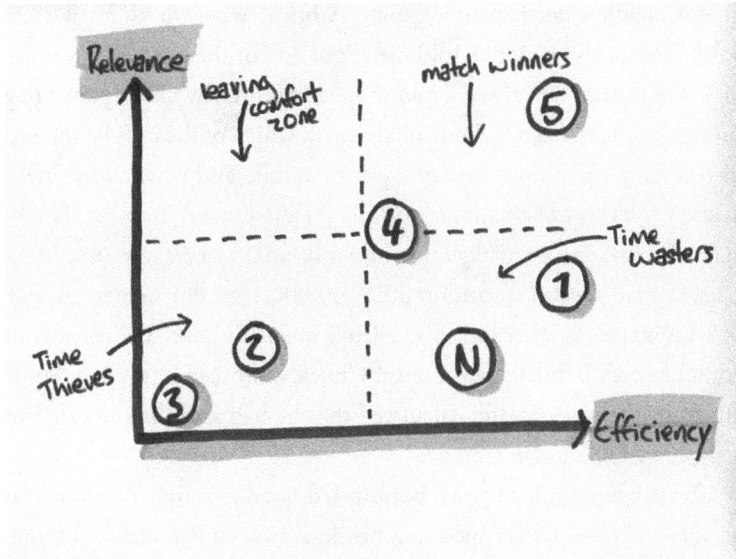

Figure 6.2 The task-relevance portfolio: matrix

Now, plot your results using the numbers from column 1 as labels onto a four-quadrant matrix, as shown in Figure 6.2. The tasks that fall in the four quadrants can now be identified as:

Time wasters;
Time thieves;
Leaving the comfort zone; or
Match winners.

This is a simple, yet surprisingly effectual mechanism that can be carried out with just a pen and pencil (once you get good at it, you will even be able to sketch the matrix in your mind, without a pen), just about where ever you like (waiting for public transport, at your desk, in a lift, and so on). It takes just a matter of seconds, but its efficacy can be powerful. The task-relevance portfolio highlights which tasks you could think about dropping, reducing, or delegating away (time thieves), which you enjoy, but could do without (time wasters), and which you should try to spend as much of your time as possible engaging in (match winners).

A Canadian participant of mine, Chuck, who works for a global player automotive supplier, told me about one of the tasks he has to perform. On the last day of every month, he is required by his employer to go through his itemized telephone bill to mark which of the calls he made on his company cell phone were of a private nature and which were strictly business. The cost of the private calls is then deducted from his monthly salary. The process normally takes him around 20 to 30 minutes. Chuck is a well-paid executive earning over 100,000 U.S. dollars per year. The time he invests in checking his cell bill normally saves his corporation around five U.S. dollars per month. Chuck went back through all of his bills from the last year and calculated that he had saved his corporation, in total, 54 U.S. dollars.

This is an example of gross, bottom-left quadrant, time thievery. Having the expensive staffer spending precious time and money fulfilling a task that he is neither talented at nor is it hugely relevant to achieving his team's goals is irresponsible and frivolous.

Mental Stress Competence

In addition to dealing with stress in an instrumental or pragmatic way, we can also take control of our pressure levels with conscious, mental control techniques. Often referred to as *reframing* (Browson 2010), appreciating your stressors and developing cognitive strategies to cope with them can be a powerful method for stress control, when developed carefully. Imagine you had a picture hanging in your apartment or house, which you had come to hate. The colors, images, and artist's techniques were not to your liking. If you were to take the picture down and have it put into a new, snazzy, attractive frame is it possible that you would look at the picture differently? The picture itself has not changed, but how you regard it has changed. In reframing, we do not change the event that is stressing us, we change how we feel about it.

Browson (2010) describes reframing as "the act of taking a situation, event, interaction et cetera. you feel negatively about and changing how you view, and thus, feel about it."

Four easy to remember reframing methods are:

Avoid, alter, adapt, accept. Adapted from Bassett (2014).

Avoid Needless Stress

You will not be able to sidestep all your stressors, but learning to say no to some external requests, averting distracting people or circumstances, and assessing the difference between *must haves* and *could haves* can help to reduce stress.

Alter Your Environment

Be strong in dealing with problems that stress you. Politely inform people that they or their actions are stressing you, instead of suppressing stressful thoughts. Increase your willingness to compromise and meet others in the middle. You cannot win all the time, and that is okay.

Adapt to the Situation

If you cannot change the stressor, change how you think about it. If something stresses you, spend more time thinking about things that bring you joy. If something appears taxing at first sight, reframe the situation to try to pick out the positives. for example, I am angry that the boss has taken me off project X—reframe to: Now I will have the time to concentrate on project Y (which I enjoy, anyway).

Accept the Way Things Are

Recognize that there are some stressors that we cannot change. Using valuable energy to fight some immovable forces is Sisyphean, in that it is futile in its nature. Instead, channel that energy to find the positives or learnings from stressful situations and accept that you have your strengths, but that no one is perfect.

One other mental stress competence is the recognition of our own ability to stress ourselves. So far, we have talked at length about external stressors (colleagues, deadlines, and so on), but lest we forget that *we* can, at times, be our own worst enemy. One of the most dangerous internal stressors can be, ironically, our own talents and strengths.

Think back to Chapter 4, where we focus comprehensively on the efficacy of recognizing our talents and using them to our advantage. What we did not consider is what happens if we exaggerate them. What happens if you overemphasize your strengths or lay them on too thick? The answer is that our strengths can become stressors, if we allow ourselves to overdo it in the strengths-based approach.

Take me as an example. Upon self-reflection, one of my strengths is my ability to communicate well. I have often received the feedback that I have a comfortable speaking style in front of a group, that I am rarely stuck for the right word, and that my active listening skills (more of this in Chapter 9) aid discourse. However, from time to time, I have also heard: "Just shut up! We get it. We've heard your voice enough today. Can you just give us a chance to think now, please without talking?" Public speaking is something I have always found easy; rhetorically I am rarely lost for the fitting word, but I do, indeed, sometimes not know when to stop. When I exaggerate on my strength of communication, it can lead to unnecessary stress as I realize that it is frustrating others.

I also consider myself adept at contextually reflecting on situations to learn from them best. But sometimes, the *context reflection machine* in my head goes into overdrive and I cannot stop thinking about what happened. Sometimes, I lie in bed at night, after a leadership workshop, turning the day just gone over and over in my head, mulling over whether I should have done this or that differently. Sometimes the *machine* runs and runs, and I end up with only five hours sleep. The lack of sleep stresses me and leaves me mentally and physically unprepared for the next day, which, in turn, again stresses me. Maybe you can see how the mental cycle of self-induced stress can quickly take its toll.

Reflect on your strengths as we mentioned in Chapter 5, but this time, consider which you may, on occasion, overdo and what stressful ramifications that may bring with it. When you have noted the potential stress-fuelling flipside of your strengths, reflect on how you can scale down their impact, using reframing and the four As technique.

Regenerative Stress Competence

The word stress literally derives from the Latin *strictus*, meaning *tight, compressed, drawn together … physical strain on a material object* (etymonline 2018). Our appreciation of the word in a psychological sense was not attributed until the 1950s. In other words, by definition, stress is a physical phenomenon, and so, as a result, we have a responsibility to our bodies to help them reduce its physical consequences.

We have the opportunity to slash stress reaction by active, physical regenerative means. According to Loehr and Schwarz (2005), the most critical and valuable resource available to any organization is its individuals' energy. Our physical energy is our fundamental source of fuel, and it affects our concentration, creativity, ability to commit, perform, and emotionally manage any given situation. Deplete our energy reservoir (through poor quantity or quality of sleep, poor diet, poor fitness levels, reduced opportunities to recover during exertion, or poor oxygen intake (i.e., breathing)) and we and our productivity suffer.

It is an old cliché, but it still rings so true: if you wanted best-in-class performance from a racing car, you would fill it with the highest-quality fuel, lubricated with the best motor oil. You would not fill up with low-grade gasoline, and you would not consider not topping up the oil as that could be damaging to all parts of the machine. You would vigorously and carefully maintain all its moving parts, keep it well-aired and in a noncorrosive environment. You would not run it at top speed all the time, you would floor the pedal only when you needed a burst of performance, but otherwise, pace the car for the long haul. In just the same way (if we expect high-performance), we have a duty of care for our bodies just as we would take care of an expensive automobile.

Our physical energy is derived from our oxygen intake and our glucose reserves (gleaned from our diet), supported by reinvigorating sleep. Resultantly, our breathing, our sleep routine, and our diet are vitally important to our well-being, performance, and stress levels. It may sound like the most obvious piece of advice you have received recently, but look after your machine!

1. Fill it up only with the highest-quality *fuel* and lubricate with the best *motor oil*, that is, balance your diet with healthy ingredients washed down with lots of water.
2. Maintain your *engine* with care, that is, practice regular, energizing, invigorating, cleansing, mindful breathing techniques.

3. Take your foot off the *gas*, that is, get lots of good-quality sleep, treat life and work as a series of sprints, not a marathon. Find hobbies, pastimes, and distractions from your work to allow you to return to your team with your batteries recharged. In order to be fully productive, we must disengage periodically and renew our focus. Just like with the sports car, we cannot run with the pedal to the metal all the time.

For the Time Management Toolbox

If I had a dollar for every time I had been asked: "Matt, how can I better manage my time?" So here, in no particular order (and this list should by no means be considered exhaustive), a quick-fire line-up of some bonus instrumental time management tips and tricks to help reduce stress and weed-out time those evil thieves:

1. Apparently, Elon Musk insists on the two-pizza rule at his companies. Musk, the billionaire businessman whose companies have given us Internet payment, fossil fuel-free cars, and who wants to take us in his rockets as space tourists into the great undiscovered, reportedly demands that no meeting at any of his companies has more attendees that can be fed by two pizzas. In other words, if two pizzas were ordered and laid out on the conference table, they would have to feed and fill up every meeting member present. If there were 16 people, it is unclear as to how much appetite Musk expects of his staff, but the principle is, I think, a clear one. If you, as a leader, are chairing a meeting or have the responsibility to invite people to a meeting, then consider in depth, who really needs to attend. On the other hand, if you are invited to a meeting to which you think you are surplus to requirements, then have the courage to say so. Excuse yourself (or, ideally, reject the invitation in advance) and allow the required attendees (and yourself) to be more productive.

2. Sync properly or do not sync at all. Sync all your calendars (including private events) to all your devices to help you keep an overview, save time asking for confirmation, and copying or blocking slots.

3. Highlight calendar entries with different colors for different roles that you have to take in the meeting to speed up your meeting preparation.

4. Use different colors for types of meetings (e.g., red for travel time, blue for sales meeting, pink for team meeting). This can save meeting preparation time.

5. To prevent bothersome, external disturbances, block personal reflection or work time, that is, slots in your calendar, that appear to colleagues that you are in a meeting, and so discouraging them from inviting you to time-wasting appointments.

6. If 4 does not work; if colleagues persist to invite you as they can see that you are the only participant in the meeting, arrange a *calendar cartel* with a friend. Both of you block the same slot, invite one another, viewers see it as a two-person meeting, and so both of you can enjoy your own personal reflection slot in peace.

7. Set e-mail reading times. Only read e-mails from 9 to 10 a.m. and from 2 to 3 p.m. Spend the rest of the time on other pursuits.

8. Set Outlook to open into the calendar screen, not into e-mail.

9. Switch e-mail notifications off. Keep your focus on the here and now.

10. One folder. Try it. Try using just one folder: a *to-do* folder. An e-mail you need to work on gets dragged to the to-do folder. Every other e-mail is left in the inbox. If you need one, use the search function. It is quicker than spending valuable time sorting e-mails into multiple, layered folders.

11. Use rules to aid your e-mail software in preorganizing your e-mails before you read them, as they come in.

12. One participant of mine revealed that he used one such rule to send any e-mail in which he was only in CC (i.e., where he was not the direct recipient) straight into trash. Time-saving, this one. But, handle with care!

13. Try teleworking, at least some of the time. It can be eye-opening how productive one can be away from the noise and distraction of the office.

14. Use digital, syncable to-do lists. They save time copying over, can be easily prioritized, (re)ordered, and collaborated on.

15. Try writing to do lists at the weekend to better streamline your household chores, to seek out a few more valuable minutes of pure relaxation time.

16. Attend a time management workshop.

17. Do not add completed items to your to-do list as you write the list, just to give yourself a mental pat on the back. It wasted three seconds writing that already completed task.

18. Elon Musk, apparently, publicly calls out inactive colleagues in meetings: He tells them that, if they are not going to contribute, then they should leave. Only attend meetings at which you can make a difference. Politely, but confidently, turn down meeting invites, which you deem time thieves.

19. For leaders, who also have a family life, try adapting to your role. Take the kids' favorite book with you on that business trip and read it over the phone to them, via video conferencing software or even send excerpts as a voice message. Give your children *family vouchers* that they can redeem when work is quieter. For example, trip to the ice cream café, game of cards, film night. With little tricks like these, working away from the family will seem less like a chore and more like an opportunity for you and your loved ones.

20. As Yves Morieux, (TED, 13:13min) puts it, "drive for clarity and accountability triggers a counterproductive multiplication of interfaces, middle offices, [and] coordinators that do not only mobilize people and resources, but that also add obstacles." Try and simplify your working environment. Eliminate as many checks, balances, and reporting functions as possible to optimize your time management, and hopefully, reduce your chances of slipping into the ugly world of stress.

Try some of these tips. They may save you some valuable minutes every day. That can add up to hours per month and days per year. Days that you could spend doing what you want to do and not stoking your flammable stress fires further.

When asked on their deathbed for their number one regret, no one answers with, *I wish I had spent more time working!* Yet, while in the rush hour of our lives, we seem determined to find any excuse available to work as much as possible. Without wanting to scare anyone, the rush hour of one's life can fly by very quickly, and before you known it, you are looking back on a life infected by stress and all the nasty ramifications it carries with it.

I will leave the last word in this chapter to the poet Joachim Ringelnatz:

You no longer smell the scent of flowers, know only work; those endless hours. Your best years go flying past, until one day you breathe your last. As you look death straight in the face, he grins and you think: what a waste.

—cited in Merg and Knödler (2005:128)[3]

Chapter Leadership Challenge

Try the task-relevance portfolio on your to-dos and invite your colleagues to do the same. Use the findings to highlight any time thieves that may be doing their evil work in your time management. Then, develop strategies to reduce their negative effect on your schedule and/or your stress levels. Drink lots of fluids, try and get as much sleep as you can (there are apps that can help, if you sometimes struggle to fall asleep), eat healthily, and try to find time for a bit of movement and/or sport, and develop a booster or enabler sentence that you can repeat to yourself, when things seem to be getting on top of you.

Mine is: *You cannot please all the people all of the time.*

---

[3] Translated by Matt Beadle from the original German by Joachim Ringelnatz.

CHAPTER 7

The Science Bit

Leaders Do Not Know About the Power of the Brain[1]

In their excellent book, *The Leading Brain*, Friederike Fabritius and Dr. Hans Werner Hagemeier (2017) note the role that our brains have in our leadership decision making.

According to Fabritius and Hagemeier, there are two key regions of the brain (Figure 7.1), whose basic makeup and effects must be understood

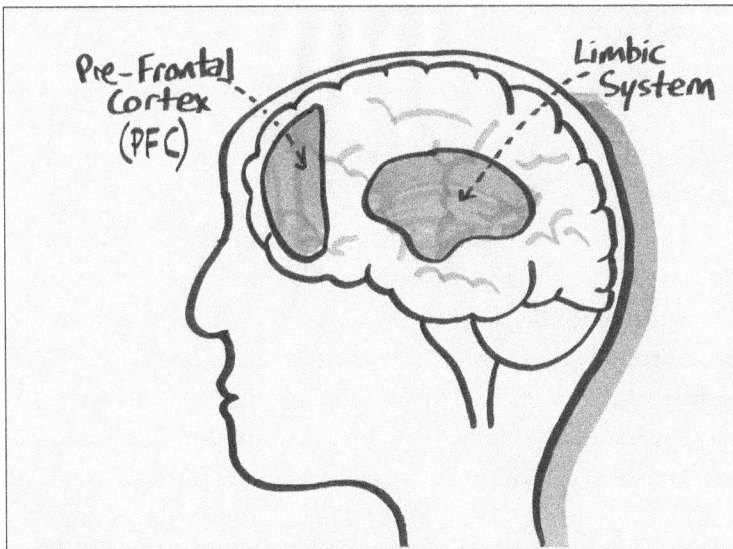

Figure 7.1 The key areas of the brain for leadership, performance, and motivation

---

[1] I am hugely grateful to Gabor Holch for his editing, advice, and input in this chapter.

by modern leaders: the prefrontal cortex (PFC) and the limbic system (LS).

Limbic System

The limbic system is the old part of the brain. It could be found in our ancestors' brains tens of thousands of years ago and is the part of the brain that deals with fundamental, basic human emotions and decisions. The challenges of our prehistoric counterparts could be described as less complex than our present-day worries, but one could argue that they regularly had to make decisions, which directly affected their (and their families') survival chances. Literally, life-and-death decisions. Dilemmas that the majority of us, on a day-to-day basis, thankfully, are not faced with today. When the saber-toothed tiger attacked, the prehistoric hunter had three opportunities: he could try to kill the animal before it killed him, he could run from the danger, or he could freeze or play dead and hope that the predator turned its attention to other prey. These three limbic responses are often referred to as:

> Fight;
> Flight; and
> Freeze.

These remain, to this day, the three main abilities of the limbic part of our brains. When danger or pressure present themselves, limbic brains quickly and inadvertently compute our survival chances and implement appropriate responses. Although the number of man-eating tigers on the streets has, thankfully, dropped significantly in recent centuries, our limbic brains are still regularly challenged to develop 21st-century *survival* options. People's decision making is, of course, also affected by their personality (nature) and their habits (nurture), but modern-day limbic responses might take the following form.

Examples:

- The boss vociferously expresses her disappointment with you, and you stand silently listening, unresponsive, apparently unable to formulate a pithy response, hoping the moment will pass. *Freeze.*

- A subordinate berates a colleague for a mistake he claims she made and she snaps back at him reminding him in no uncertain words of the dreadful performance he delivered in the last project. *Fight.*

- For a while, you have been intending to arrange a one-on-one with a member of your team to discipline them for their recent, poor performance, but you have put off scheduling the appointment a number of times because you *do not feel ready*. *Flight.*

When our brains receive input and stimuli that requires computation—for example, we see or hear something (not if we burn ourselves for example)—it first arrives at the receptors at the back of the brain before it is sent to the limbic system. This is the first part of the brain that deconstructs what it has detected, and it has two distinct modes in which it can function: *reward mode* and *threat mode* (Fabritius and Hagemann 2017). If the stimulus is deemed dangerous or threatening, then threat mode drives on, the powerful hormone cortisol is released, and the system goes into survival mode. The brain switches on any parts of the physiological complex it deems necessary for survival and inhibits those it presumes surplus to existential requirements. However, if the brain registers the impulse as nonthreatening, then the signal is diverted to the PFC where it is analyzed in greater detail, and with support from the hormone dopamine, rational cognition fires up. Unfortunately, evolution has trained us to be in threat mode as our default setting. Our first instinct is to protect ourselves, and when working in threat mode, cortisol is in the ascendancy.

But, our reaction to stress situations is not only cerebral. In threat mode, along with dopamine, the brain also releases the hormone noradrenaline, which can be thought of as the messenger to the body to switch to survival mode. When we are under stress, we often notice uncomfortable physiological reactions in addition to the stunted deductive skills we experience. Think of a time when you felt under pressure, under stress, in a powerfully nervous state or scared or unsure of a situation. Before an exam, in the period leading up to an important deadline, moments before a job interview, for example. At such junctures, we often experience some or all of the following in our bodies: clammy or cold hands, racing or uneven heart rate, sweating, a sick feeling or *butterflies* in our stomach, fidgety hands and feet, flushed skin, and others. This physiological activity is nothing more than the body switching to threat mode and protecting itself.

Think back to the flight/fight/freeze status. When faced with such plight, the brain is not the only organ that switches on survival mode; the body is prepared for to protect itself too. The brain, with the help of noradrenaline, diverts energy away from the parts of the body which it deems less necessary in times of danger, and toward systems that will need blood, oxygen, glucose, and all the chemicals we need to fuel ourselves in precarious times. To transport these goodies to the areas in need, noradrenaline drives up heart activity, making it pump more blood faster around the body; this is why, our heart races when we are nervous or stressed. The brain deems the stomach less important (we can go weeks without food in times of crisis), so activity in and energy to the digestive system is reduced with the valuable fuel sent to parts more in need; this digestive shutdown sometimes feels like butterflies in the stomach. Our clammy, fidgety appendages are preparing for fight and feel as such as they receive less blood than normal with it being diverted to major muscle groups needed to run and defend (i.e., the legs and arms). And, I have sadly watched many nervous students' faces flush deep red during university examinations—this being also a reaction to the body's frenetic diversion of blood to key areas. All in all, threat mode (and its ubiquitous hormones cortisol and noradrenaline) puts a great demand on our cognitive and physiological state, and its effects and symptoms should not be underestimated by aware leaders.

The limbic system's alternate mode, however, is reward mode. Driven by the hormone dopamine (the happiness hormone that gives us a kick when thrill seeking), reward mode opens up creative centers in the brain that help us to work in a positive, original manner.

If it was a matter of choice, I think most of us would simply switch on reward mode, flood the system with the fun hormone dopamine, and spend our days being innovative and productive (and probably with a big smile on our faces). Unfortunately, it is not as easy as that. Sadly, we do not have direct control over our untrained brain. Threat mode is on as default and we cannot just switch parts of the brain on and off at our pleasure. Regular, focused, mindful, and determined self-reflection is required to train our brains to work more in reward mode. Furthermore, cortisol is stronger and lingers in our brain nine times longer than dopamine, so reversing the control of cortisol is very hard for us (Fabritius and Hagemann, 2017). Want as we may to believe that we are in cognitive control over all our adjudicature, it is often the chemicals which hold the upper hand.

However, there is another issue.

Prefrontal Cortex

The other key part of the leader's brain is the PFC. Sitting proudly in the front of our heads, it is the younger part of the brain that humans have only developed in the last few thousand years. We share this part of the brain with only a few other animals (including dolphins and apes). It is the exciting hub of rational, objective, inventive thought, and its size and cognitive power are what separates us from our cousins in the animal kingdom. Our developed PFCs have helped us build the astonishing, interconnected world we live in today. It allowed us to think up the engines that power the cars on our roads, to calculate the science that has allowed us to put planes in the sky, to discover cures for thousands of microbial diseases, and every other great accomplishment that we, as the human race, have achieved. The PFC is the site of rational cognition. Unfortunately, as I mentioned before, there is an issue, namely that:

The PFC reduces activity when we are in threat mode.

In other words, when we find ourselves under stress in pressure situations, cortisol streams through our system, fueling threat mode in the limbic system and blocking the PFC from helping us consider the options rationally, objectively, and intellectually. So, when the boss screams at us, the deadline rears its ugly head all too fast, or the potential client pulls out of a huge deal; snatching from you the bonus that you had already spent on that sofa, rational thought is very difficult (the PFC is largely inactive), and threat mode and the cortisol of the limbic system are in control. We revert to our prehistoric tendencies; fight, flight, or freeze. What is more, the PFC guzzles hundreds of times the glucose that the limbic system requires, but when the PFC is inhibited, some of the glucose is diverted to the LS, starving the PFC of the energy it needs to aid rational focus.

The perfect example of a situation where the PFC seemed inhibited and the cortisol-fueled LS apparently in command, was in the soccer world cup final game between France and Italy in 2006. The Frenchman Zenedine Zidane, for many at the time the greatest player in the world, playing in his last game for his country after a glittering career, inexplicably and suddenly turned and head-butted his opponent, the Italian Marco Materazzi, in the middle of the field, in clear view of all spectators and the match officials (Guardian 2007). Zidane was subsequently shown the red card and ejected from the game. His team, France, duly went on to lose the game on penalty kicks. Ironic, as Zidane had a record as a world-class penalty taker, and had he remained on the pitch, very possibly might have helped his team win the match.

The rational, focused, intelligent action in that moment would have been to have ignored the alleged insults from his opponent (Guardian 2007) and to have continued playing, utilizing all of his significant skills and talents to help his team win the game and his country the world cup. But, Zidane was probably not thinking clearly at that moment, that is, his PFC was almost certainly not fully switched on. His system was in threat mode, cortisol was doing its dastardly hormonal work, and his LS propelled him (literally) to fight against what it deemed a genuine threat. Whatever stimulated him to slip into threat, mode we do not know, but the lack of rational thought at an otherwise hugely important moment was conspicuous by its absence, and the prevalence of pure survival fight instinct powerfully apparent. So you can see, even the greats experience moments, where threat mode presides.

In threat mode, we all react in different ways. Some panic, overreact, overwork, or lash out. Some cover-up their feelings, some turn to other stimulants and satisfiers such as alcohol, tobacco, or calories, some bottle-up deep-lying beliefs and thoughts for fear of recrimination, some run from their responsibilities. Some are confrontational and seem to seek conflict at any opportunity. Many react differently again (Demptser 2012). Whatever the symptoms, the root cause in labor-induced stress scenarios is almost always a stunted PFC; the cerebral system flooded with cortisol; an LS in threat mode, that is, in fight, flight, or freeze status; and so a lack of cognitive control and rationality.

In addition to the mental stress we put ourselves under when we are in threat mode, there are very real and potentially damaging physiological effects that the overload of cortisol in the system can lead to. Chronic cortisol release, over years of working in stressful situations in threat mode, has been shown to reduce hippocampal functionality (Sheline et al. 1996) and an underperforming hippocampus (a further part of the brain) has been connected with a host of medical conditions, including (but not limited to) memory loss (Luipen et al. 1994), severe weight loss (Pelleymounter, Cullen, and Wellman 1995), and immune system dysfunction. (Dantzer, R., O'Connor et al. 2008). Notably, a number of studies have also reported a direct correlation between the onset of burnout and heightened levels of somatic cortisol. (Melamed et al. 1999; Joyce, Mulder, and Cloninger 1994). So, the dangers of threat mode are threefold.

1. We stand a far greater chance of reacting to an otherwise soluble challenge irrationally.
2. Noradrenaline puts our bodies under increased physiological pressure.
3. We run the risk of serious, deep-rooted medical problems if we subject ourselves to lasting cortisol release.

Fighting Back Against Fight or Flight or Freeze

Your people, when under stress or in conflict, are not only disappointed that their needs are not being met at a micro or macro level, but their actions are also strongly chemically driven. Hormones, synapses and millennia of genetic training stimulates them to react (both physiologically and mentally) as they do. Your responsibility as a leader is to free people from the red mist of limbic subordination and get them back to the rationality of PFC supremacy.

According to Klaus Dürrbeck (2018), there is a program of options available to leaders to help their associates switch on reward mode, and they can be handily subdivided into short- and longer-term adjustments:

Short-Term Measures *(Prerequisite Is that the Person Under Stress Is Aware that They Are in Threat Mode)*

1. **Combat breathing**: Four cycles, repeated as long as required. Long, slow intakes of breath (four seconds). Hold (four seconds). Long, slow exhale (four seconds). Through such breathing execution, one is able to focus attention on the technique itself and away from the threatening subject. One's heart rate is also slowed in a controlled manner and one's parasympathetic nervous system (the division of your autonomic nervous system, closest to the brain and responsible for guiding the body in times of rest) engages and relaxes you.[2]

2. **Avoid inhibition**: Attempting to consciously suppress one's threat reactions can lead to exhausting the PFC's limited energy resources (glucose). Do not think of a pink elephant! We all immediately cannot think of anything else, other than a pink elephant, now. And the same applies to threat mode. When you try tell yourself not to be in threat mode, you think more about threat mode. Instead:

3. **Labeling**: Describe the threat or emotions in your own words. Giving the bugbear a name helps it to appear less threatening. One feels more in control. For example, when faced with a project cancelation from a client, resulting in threatened financial independence, name it: "This is bad situation. I have had the rug pulled from under my feet." After having labeled the threat, the next step could be:

4. **Reinterpretation or reappraisal**: (Requires practice) identify and emphasize the positives from the negatives ("the situation with the client has shown me that I have a weakness in my client network/in my business model, that I can now improve on!")

5. **Conscious (paradox) intervention** from another person *(targeted distraction)*. To channel attention away from the threat subject. "Where did you last go on holiday to?" "What did Stephen say to you after in that meeting the other day?"

6. **Physical activity:** The pent up energy has to have a release for examples through a walk in the fresh air, 30 squats, 20 push-ups, and so on.

---

[2] The technique originates from a Special Forces soldier, who trained himself to relax in situations of extreme stress in action in Afghanistan.

7. **Metacognition**: (Requires practice) reflect over one's own thought patterns and reactions to draw farther and farther away in order to take an external position. Reduces stress and opens up new perspectives.

8. **Appreciative recognition or *Permission* from manager**: Sometimes, it can help to show a subordinate that the superior recognizes and can appreciate his or her (threat) reactions and to clarify that it is okay to feel under pressure or feel stress, at times. For example, "In your situation, it is ok to feel like you have been treated unfairly." Such action breeds an atmosphere of emotional appreciation and recognition.

Long-Term Measures

1. **Mindfulness** techniques: such techniques help people to tolerate more arousal or stress before they *slip* into threat mode. At the same time, they allow you to recognize faster when a threat is approaching, so allowing you to instigate short-term measures before you fall down the rabbit hole.

2. **Emotional self-regulation**: Practice and implement.

3. **Establishing a fear-free climate** through consistent use of the *SCARF* model:
   *S*tatus: How do I gauge my relative importance to others.
   *C*ertainty: How good am I at predicting the future.
   *A*utonomy: How strong is my perceived sense of control over events.
   *R*elatedness: My sense of comfort, when working with others (friends rather than foes).
   *F*airness: How fairly do I perceive exchanges between people.

4. Awareness of which factors I require for **peak performance**: am I the kind of person who requires (time) pressure to achieve top performance or do I fall easily and uncontrollably into threat mode? Understand your own hormonal release and balance. Seek medical advice.

5. **Regular sport**: Sport or physical activity of any sort heightens your stress tolerance and burns-off energy otherwise stored to fuel threat mode and helps to regulate cortisol levels, thus reducing potential buildup of somatic cortisol and preventing chronic stress.

6. **Sufficient sleep**: Chronic sleep deprivation increases susceptibility to stress.

Chapter Leadership Challenge

Our challenge as a leader is to try to facilitate a positive working and communicative environment so that potential conflicts and stress can be avoided by offering a harmonious setting, where colleagues can work positively and with creativity in reward mode.

If you feel that a process partner, or indeed you, are stuck in threat mode and unable to act intellectually with the PFC, then try introducing new stimuli to challenge their brains to compute new information. This should lead to them switch on their PFC to interpret the new challenge, so reducing the damaging control that the cortisol and limbic system were having.

Keep a retrospective diary of moments, when you noticed the red mist settling in and try to record what triggered threat mode, in the first place. Develop strategies to avoid such red zones in the future.

CHAPTER 8

The Big Battle

Leaders Often Apply the Wrong Leadership Style

Leadership Styles

Enough has been written about leadership styles over the years to fill a library. Indeed, Stogdill (1974) japed that "there are almost as many different definitions of leadership as there are persons who have attempted to define the concept." Dubrin (2000) claims the number of definitions for leadership might be in the region of 35,000. Furthermore, opinions seem to differ as to which is the best style to apply to any given leadership situation. Fads and trends come and go. In any given leadership zeitgeist, this or that style could to be in vogue. All of which makes it difficult for the future manager to grasp a memorable snapshot that will help him or her with the nuance of delegation.

Scholars pose multiple renderings of what leadership is or should be.[1] Let us take a look at some:

Northouse (2004) claims it "is a process… involves influence… occurs in group context… involves goal attainment." Yukl (2002) defines it as "the process of influencing others to understand and agree what needs to be done and how to do it, and the process of facilitating individual and collective efforts to accomplish shared objectives." Whereas, according to Goffee and Jones (2006) "Leadership is about results. Great leadership has the potential to excite people to extraordinary levels of achievement. But it is not only about performance; it is also about meaning. Leaders at all levels make a difference to performance. They do so because they make

---

[1] My thanks to Michael Knieling for his contribution to this collection of quotes.

performance meaningful." Kouzes and Posner (1995) see leadership as "the art of mobilizing others to want to struggle for shared aspirations," while Van Vugt, Hogan, and Kaiser (2008) see it more pragmatically in their definition of leadership as "…(a) influencing individuals to contribute to group goals and (b) coordinating the pursuit of those goals." Some similar themes here, but little concrete accord from the theorists.

Maybe the practitioners have been able to come to a more centralized understanding of leadership.[2]

(a) "The leaders who work most effectively, it seems to me, never say "I"." Peter Drucker, Management Guru. (1909–2005) (cited by Lipman 2018)

(b) "Be realistic, demand the impossible!" Che Guevara, Cuban revolutionist. (1928–1967) (cited in hey-che.com 2017)

(c) "Before you are a leader, success is all about growing yourself. When you become a leader, success is all about growing others." Jack Welch, former CEO General Electric.

(d) "…have the courage to disrupt old structures!" Jürgen Klinsmann, former German Soccer head coach. (Cited by Jenewein 2008).

(e) "In matters of style, swim with the current; in matters of principle, stand like a rock." Thomas Jefferson. 3rd president of the United States. (1743–1826)

(f) "A leader is a dealer in hope." Napoleon Bonaparte. French statesman (1769–1821)

(g) "The art of leadership is saying no, not saying yes. It is very easy to say yes." Tony Blair, former British Prime Minister.

(h) "As we look ahead into the next century, leaders will be those who empower others." Bill Gates. Founder of Microsoft.

(i) "Leadership and learning are indispensable to each other." John F. Kennedy. (35th president of the United States. (1917–1963)

A hop through some historical quotes on leadership further exposes the discordance of sentiment to leadership styles. My intention was not to cloud the issue here; apologies if I have done that. What I hoped to show you is the sheer variety of stances on leadership offered to us, both from

---

[2] C, e, f, g, h, i cited by Kruse (2012).

academics and practicing leaders, over the ages. One thing is clear: they cannot all be right. And, they are certainly not all wrong.

As Jefferson touches on in his quote, one's leadership style is irrefutably associated to one's own principles and beliefs (see Chapter 2), but it is also the managing of processes together with people (Kouzes and Posner 1995; 2010), and at the same time, varied and situational (as intimated by Kennedy and Jobs).

Leadership is situationally adjusting your approach to people in order to get their best out of them.

We can learn a lot from role models (both positive and negative). We have already heard from Bill Gates. Let us take a closer look at his leadership style. Gates is a singularly focused and determined individual (Gilliard, n.d.), who, as the head of Microsoft, worked long hours and expected the same dedication from his team (Rampton 2016). He believed in pursuing what you love and working in a field that stimulates you. He was a once-in-a-generation subject knowledge expert (software coding). He is shy and introverted, but polite and well-mannered. He made decisions quickly, was autocratic and authoritarian, but encouraged his team to challenge the status quo with new ideas, although he often chastised them for what he deemed inaccurate assumptions or incorrect facts (Chris 2015). He was not necessarily an ideas guy (for example, he bought the operating system BASIC, he did not actually create it), but his anticipation of trends was first rate. Since stepping back from direct control of Microsoft, he has set up the largest private foundation in the United States, the Bill and Melinda Gates Foundation, which aims to reduce poverty with multi-billion-dollar philanthropy.

At around the same time that Bill Gates was making waves in the software industry, a young college dropout was nudging his technologically more-gifted friend Steve Wozniak to develop the world's first attractive home computer in his parents' garage. Steve Jobs became a fiery, and fiercely ambitious leader, who surrounded himself with talent and pushed them to ever greater creative achievements (Isaacson 2012). This persuasive force that Jobs wielded was jokingly referred to as his "Reality Distortion Field after an episode of Star Trek in which aliens create a convincing alternative reality through sheer mental force" (Isaacson 2012). For example, he was once able to convince Steve Wozniak to design a game for Atari in four days, although Wozniak claimed he needed months. He has been described as "arrogant, dictatorial, and mean-spirited" (Henson 2011), but was a genius with regards to design, did not care for customer or popular opinion "customers don't know what they want until we've shown them" (Isaacson 2012), and was an extroverted, salesman-supreme with the rare gift of the gab and unequalled persuasive, sales and pitching techniques (Isaacson 2011). In his private life, Gates was reclusive and stubborn. He estranged himself from family members for decades and lived in a sparsely decorated house, often sitting on the floor for lack of furniture.

Two men. Born around the same time. Growing up in the same period of history. Brought up in similar, American, middle-class backgrounds. Both entered the same (burgeoning computer) industry, and both went on to become captains of industry, founding leaders of two of the most successful companies (by capital and market share) the world has ever seen. But, both worked and led in very different ways. Jobs achieved greatness with silky communication skills and raw (but strengths-oriented) emotion, whereas Gates' drive, blinkered determination (he never let 21 years of legal challenges distract his work) and subject matter skills helped him lead his company to the top. Jobs' leadership gathered creative experts (he was never considered a computer expert himself) into his close circle of followers and drove them to excellence with ceaseless and seductive persuasion. Gates, on the other hand, founded his leadership philosophy on his own subject skills combined with tireless focus and attention to detail. He rarely included others in decision making and micromanaged every aspect of business. However, his philanthropic nature was conspicuous in comparison to Jobs' troublesome private relationships.

Two unforgettable leaders with two very distinct leadership styles.

There is no golden road to leadership success. Leadership is situational and varied. What *is* true is that, whichever style you choose, it will fall somewhere on the following leadership spectrum.

Transformational Versus Transactional Leadership

If we were on a sinking ship, how might the crew communicate with the passengers?

(a) "Dear, respected passenger. I trust you are having a pleasant journey with us. As you might have noticed, the ship is sinking and anyone not in the lifeboats will surely drown. I would like to invite you to reflect on whether or not you would like to climb into a lifeboat of your choice. It is your decision which one you take. It is also your choice as to when you board the lifeboat. I trust you to make the right decision and am there to assist should you need any help."

(b) *Get in that lifeboat, now!*

There is a time and place for the leadership style portrayed in a. (transformational leadership), and we will cover that in detail later in the chapter. But, it is hugely important for young leaders to recognize that b. (transactional leadership) is still a completely valid and often suitable choice for *certain* leadership scenarios. Firefighters, the armed forces, the police force, medical teams, situations involving safety (for example, involving children), inexperienced newcomers, and many others experience powerful transactional leadership on a daily basis. When leading a team of firefighters required to rush into a burning building or leading a team of nurses and doctors trying to save the life of a dying patient, democratic, transformational, decision making by committee is time-wasting, can lead to protocols and regulations being broken, and could ultimately end in tragedy. However, in challenging situations regarding creativity, elaborate cognition, and intellect (see Chapter 7), expression of talent (see Chapter 4) and to drive motivation and personal development (see Chapter 5), transformational leadership is essential (Gumusluoglu and Ilsev 2009).

What is interesting is that nature does not appear to prefer either one definitive leadership approach. Both seem to have their place. The chimpanzee and the bonobo monkey (close relatives genetically) have been observed to lead their troops very differently from one another. The dominant chimpanzee in the group commands his or followers in a (transactional) direct, aggressive, and controlling style. The structure of the troop is strictly top-down and hierarchical. But, this differs greatly from the network structure seen in bonobo monkeys. They protect and assist each other (whether dominant male or otherwise) and appear to work together for the common good, without an obvious, hierarchy (transformational)

(Wrangham and Peterson 1996). The only learning we could take from our ape cousins is that both species live in different environments, and so might have needed to develop differing survival tactics.

Both leadership styles exist in the animal and human kingdoms. So, now let us take a closer look at the two ends of the leadership styles spectrum.

Transactional leadership, metaphorically speaking, keeps things ticking along; it keeps the ship afloat. Transactional leaders instruct, command, set goals, and expect them to be completed and reward and motivate accordingly. Hence, the term transactional (Ingram 2018). This type of leader reduces their relationship with their team, by way of their disciplinary power, to a series of transactions. "I would like you to complete X by next week…. Do this on time and you will get that reward…" Transactional leaders are more concerned with the status quo of procedures and work less toward strategic or developmental organizational or personal change. The difference between transactional and transformational leadership is what the leader and follower offer each other (Conger and Kanungo 1998). Transactional leadership offers the follower targets, clarity and rewards whereby transformational leadership offers the follower significantly more.

The term transformational leadership is first accredited to James Burns in 1978 (Judge and Piccolo 2004), was later refined by Bass (1985, 1995) and describes a leadership style that facilitates personal development of followers through charismatic, supportive, encouraging, coaching, motivating, rewarding, inspiring, intellectually stimulating, and appropriate promotional rhetoric and action. Bass and Riggio (2006) highlight four key areas (known as the 4Is) on which a transactional leader focuses, and ultimately, develops his or her followers:

Idealized influence (II): The leader serves as an ideal role model for followers; the leader "walks the talk," and is admired for this.

Inspirational motivation (IM): Transformational leaders have the ability to inspire and motivate followers. Combining these first two Is constitutes the transformational leader's charisma.

Individualized consideration (IC): Transformational leaders demonstrate genuine concern for the needs and feelings of followers. This personal attention to each follower is a key element in bringing out their very best efforts.

Intellectual stimulation (IS): The leader challenges followers to be innovative and creative. A common misunderstanding is that transformational leaders are "soft," but the truth is that they constantly challenge followers to higher levels of performance (Riggio 2009).

Yukl (1994) builds on the 4Is with tips for transformational leaders:

1. Develop an inspirational and exciting vision, together with your team.
2. Tie the vision to a strategy for its achievement.
3. Develop the vision, specify and translate it to actions.
4. Express confidence, decisiveness, and optimism about the vision and its implementation.
5. Realize the vision through small planned steps and small successes in the path for its full implementation.

Transformational leadership feeds from strengths-oriented communication (Chapter 4), intrinsic motivational techniques (Chapter 5), shared vision and purpose (Chapter 2), and reward mode in the brain (Chapter 8), and has been shown by numerous studies to increase employee engagement, innovation. and productivity (Dong, Chow, and Wu, 2003; Gumusluoglu and Ilsev 2009; Wang et al. 2011; Pieterse et al. 2010; Anderson, Potočnik, and Zhou 2014).

However, it is important that you think of these two leadership styles as being interconnected, not distinct from one another. You may instinctively favor one style over the other, but that does not mean that you cannot employ both at different moments. Your challenge will be to find the *mix* of styles and adapt and adjust according to the situation at hand. On some occasions, you will require a more transactional tack, while at other times, you will be better served by leading transformationally.

Situational Leadership

Which leadership style I apply to any given situation is dependent on:

- The experience of the associate;
- The knowledge of the associate;
- The complexity of the task at hand;
- The timing with regards to other projects;
- Previous transactions with this associate;
- Future, desired dynamic in the team;
- Type and complexity of task;
- The culture in the organization,… and countless other factors.

In other words, to lead effectively, you will need to lead situationally. If you try and fix every problem with a hammer, you will break a lot of wood. Some situations require hammers, but many call for other tools. The term situational leadership was coined by management researchers Hersey and Blanchard (1977) and in their approachable and easy-to-remember leadership styles model, they suggest four approaches by the leader, each situationally applicable to specific cases.

Situational leadership places the leader's behavior onto two axes: directive and supportive. Directive behavior describes the extent to which the leader spells out the role of the associate; tells the associate what to do, how to do it, where to do it, and by when; uses one-way communication; and supervises performance attentively. A leader engaging in strongly directive behavior sets the goals and objectives alone, plans and structures associate workload, checks on progress, sets and reviews scheduling, determines how success will be evaluated, clarifies both his or her and the associates' rules and roles, and regularly communicates priorities.

Supportive behavior can be defined as the extent to which the leader engages in two-way communication, facilitates associate interaction, involves the associate in decision making, listens, and offers help and motivation. A supportive leader invites ideas and suggestions, praises success, shares information, listens to associates' issues (private or professional), keeps the associates up to date regarding the organization's operations, and encourages problem-solving attitudes (Graeff 1983).

When we place the directive behavior on the X axis (from low to high) and the supportive behavior on the Y axis (low to high) (Figure 8.1), we can identify four key areas of leadership style: telling (known as S1), guiding (S2), anticipating (S3), and delegating (S4).

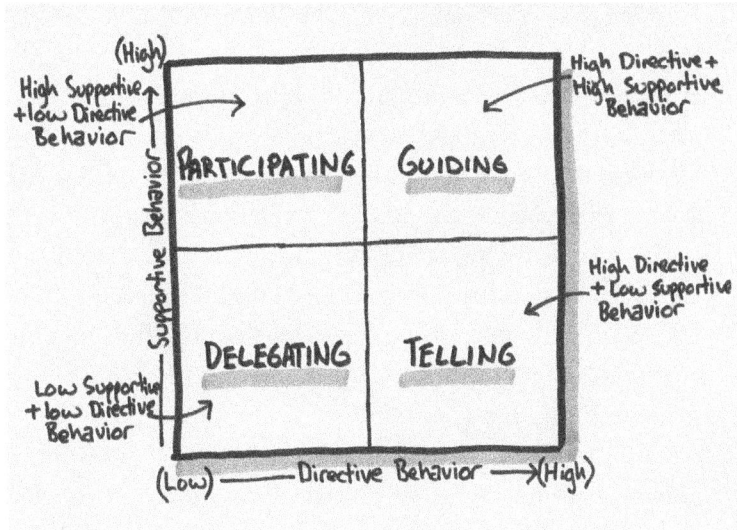

Figure 8.1 Situational leadership model

The situational leader applies the fitting leadership style and adjusts when necessary. Situational leadership requires patience, and you will need to finely tune your *antenna* to quickly and adeptly assess which manner is the most apt. Situational leadership is fair, strengths-oriented, and transformational.

Leading Teams

A phenomenon that many leaders note is that leading *teams* is far more complex than leading individuals. In the current chapter, we have looked in detail at different leadership styles and the skill of situationally applying them, but we have yet to refer those leadership skills to teams.

In his now seminal work, Bruce Tuckman (1965), looked at 55 studies into group development and noticed a pattern in the ways the teams grew, collaborated, and developed together. On the back of that study, Tuckman (1965) developed a solid four-stage model,[3] which has been substantially used to describe typical phases of team development, ever since. According to Tuckman (1965), the stages are:

---

[3] With a 5th phase—adjourning—added in 1977 (Tuckman and Jensen).

1. **Forming phase**: Roles and responsibilities are often unclear, and the team uses a large amount of energy getting to know one another. People use this phase as orientation. Behavior is usually well-mannered, but many team members act individually and for their own best interests. Most of the focus is on understanding the task at hand and on developing the beginnings of an approach strategy.

   The team depends greatly, in this first phase, on their leader for guidance and direction. There is usually little agreement on aims, apart from those set by the leader. In the forming phase, the leader often has to apply a directive, transactional leadership style.

   Leader directs and coordinates.

2. **Storming phase**: As the title suggests, this can be a turbulent period in team development. As the following image shows (Figure 8.2), teams in the storming phase often experience a perceived drop in

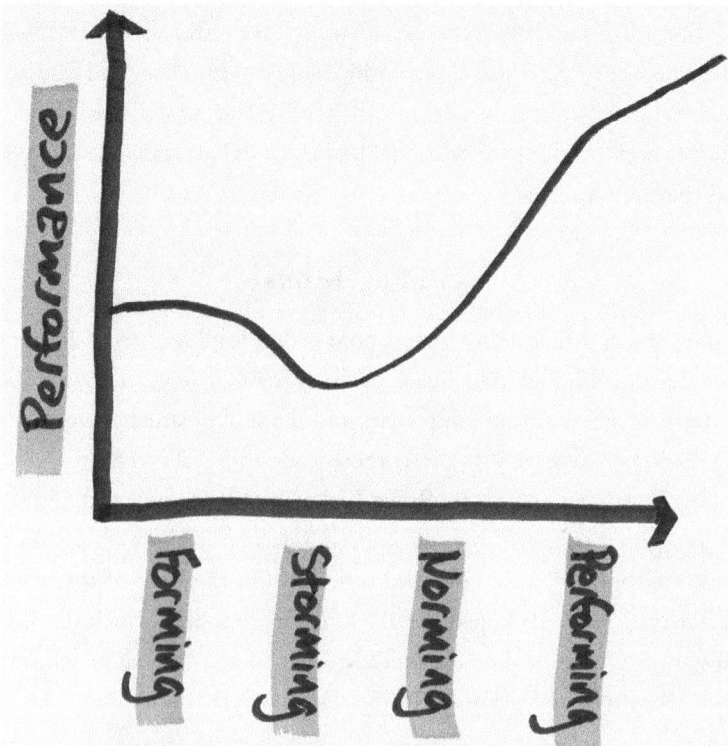

Figure 8.2 The phases of team development according to Tuckman

measurable, immediate performance as focus is distracted away from executing and toward challenging the status quo and into discussion. Members of teams in the storming phase raise contrasting ideas, and this difference of opinion can lead to conflict as colleagues vie for position and often compete with one another. Cliques and sub-groups develop as people struggle for power and control. However, the storming phase can be described as cathartic for many.

The leader has to tread carefully in this phase to ensure that the team members do not get distracted from their goals by relation-ship issues or conflicts. A challenge of the leader will be to assist the group in finding compromises. The leader will have to solve emo-tional issues before the group can progress to its next level of team development. Tuckman did note, though, that only around half of the groups experience a storming phase at all, with the other 50 per-cent jumping straight to phase 3. If the leadership motto in phase 1 is *direct*, then it is *coach* in stage 2.

Leader coaches and supports.

3. **Norming phase**: Once teams can get over the potential hurdle of the storming phase, they are rewarded with the norming phase, where performance levels explode and teams find their feet. Whims and idiosyncrasies of team members are appreciated and accepted. A new-found consensus allows teams to focus on its goals and pro-cesses, with little need for leadership directive and without the bag-gage of interpersonal disputes. The team develops autonomy. Smaller decisions and tasks might be delegated to small groups, but major accord is achieved by the whole.

The leader often experiences respect from his or her team in the norming phase. With team members aware of the roles and respon-sibilities, the feeling of affiliation grows and teams often engage in social activities together. As direction is steered by the group, the leader employs a more transformational approach in this phase and delegates to individuals or groups.

Leader empowers, facilitates, and enables.

4. **Performing phase**: Teams in the 4th stage are knowledgeable, expe-rienced, and energized by successes in the forming phase. Team members are more strategically informed; each knows their role, and

a vision is shared. The autonomy levels are high which facilitates solving disagreements, with ease and with little disruption to overall goals. Decisions can be made without leadership involvement, which speeds up process and strengthens the feeling of achievement and self-worth. This in turn, leads to greater quality of performance.

Leaders in the performing stage can reduce their leadership to such a level that they often merely participate with the team. The leader need only delegate tasks and might be asked for assistance from the team, but goals are understood and need not be recommunicated by the leader.

Leader delegates and assists, where required.

What becomes obvious is that both works from Tuckman (1965) and Hershey and Blanchard (1977) are four-stage models, and they can, indeed (Table 8.1), be combined to provide helpful guidance to the young leader on which leadership style to situationally apply to teams at each stage of their development.

Table 8.1 Team phases and leadership styles. Adapted from Manges et al. (2017)

Team development stage	Leadership strategies	Keys to success
Forming	Coordinating behaviors (Telling S1)	-Purposefully picking the team -Facilitate team to identify goals -Ensure the team development of a shared mental model
Storming	Coaching behaviors (Guiding S2)	-Act as a resource person to the team -Develop mutual trust -Calm the work environment
Norming	Empowering behaviors (Participating S3)	-Get feedback from staff -Allow for the transfer of leadership -Set aside time for planning and engaging the team -Allow for flexibility in team roles
Performing	Supporting behaviors (Delegating S4)	-Assist in the timing and selection of new member -Create future leadership opportunities

Chapter Leadership Challenge

Sit down and reflect on where you stand on the 4Is. What do you do to act as a role model? How do you inspire the people around you? Do you treat people individually and manage situationally? Do you delegate appropriate to intellectual ability, or do you give the guy with the MBA the most menial of tasks? What areas of the 4Is could you work on? Set yourself some targets, and try to develop your transformational leadership.

Take a snapshot in your mind, or on paper, as to where your team currently is with regards to the team phases (forming, storming, norming, and performing). Once you have done that, consider what your team would need and how you as a leader can facilitate moving them onto the next phase.

CHAPTER 9

Persuasive Communication

Many Good Leaders Do Not Use Convincing-Enough Rhetoric

Universals of Persuasion

There are times when a leader may have to call up some persuasive skills, for example, to get others on board with a new direction or to align associates with new strategy. Despite increasing use of transformational leadership in corporations, many decisions are still taken at higher-hierarchy levels with department heads, and team leaders then charged with the task of disseminating the information, and should the need arise, convincing associates of the benefits of the change.

For instance, if the management board had introduced a new benefits scheme for its sales force, whereby instead of a purely intrateam, competitive model with the sales person with the best sales figures reaping all the bonus remuneration, the whole team benefitted from targets met, then the manager would be faced with the challenge of trying to persuade the hitherto high-earners of the new scheme's virtues. Maybe your team has expressed apprehension about entering a particular new market or at the success chances of introducing a new model or product range. Or, maybe some of the team have approached, requesting free language classes and the leader agrees to fund the training program, but requests, in return, that the classes take place either early in the morning or later in the evening—out of the office time. That is, in the workers' own spare time. In any of these situations, persuasive rhetoric would be helpful for the leader.

We have a tendency as a species to be weary of change, so do not be surprised if you encounter resistance when presenting such new strategic proposals to your team. In such cases, fair, transparent, informative

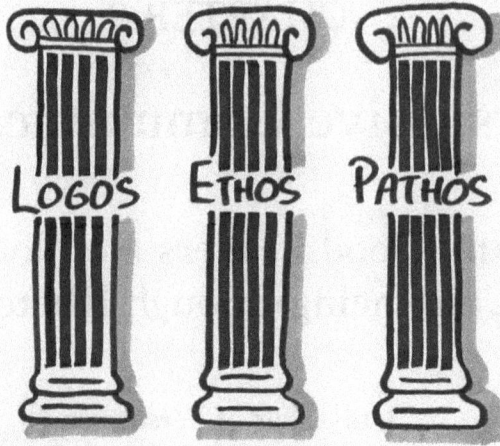

Figure 9.1 The three Aristotlean pillars of rhetoric

communication is the order of the day, combined with some useful persuasive techniques.

Aristotle introduced us to the power of persuasion a couple of
millennia ago (Freese 1926), yet its tenets still ring powerfully true today
(Figure 9.1). According to Aristotle, there are three essentials pillars to
convincing (persuasive) communication:

Logos can be thought of as the argument itself, the details, the foci,
logical reasoning, what many today would refer to as the benefits or the
USP (Higgins and Walker 2010). But, even the soundest, most objective
arguments lack persuasive power if they are not presented in a way that
commands respect. If the speaker is not considered authoritative and to
have credibility, then what he or she is saying can also be disregarded,
irrespective of its logic or truth. Aristotle referred to this as *ethos*. (See also
Authority, next). And, thirdly, Aristotle's *pathos* is the feeling, emotion,
and style in which the speaker communicates (Demirdöğen 2010).

All in all, Aristotle's principles of rhetoric can be collated to make a
helpful formula for developing persuasive communication.

Audience + Purpose + Genre = Style (how it is presented) + content
(what is said)

For example: If a group of students wanted to complain about the canteen food, which method of communication might be more effective?

(a) They write a letter to the person responsible for the catering.
(b) They stage a protest in the canteen.

Probably the latter.

Put another way: consider who you are communicating with, what you aim to achieve, and what the background is, and then decide on *what* you say and *how* you want to say it, accordingly.

Developing upon Aristotle's three pillars, Dr. Robert Cialdini, in his multimillion selling book: *Influence, the Power of Persuasion* (2006), highlights six universal principles of persuasion.

1. Reciprocity: People are likely to feel more obliged do something for people in return for something that they have done for them in the past.

   In other words, we tend to return favors to those who have already helped us. It is deeply human and can be traced back to the need felt by our ancestors to support each other in tribal groups. For example, one cooks, one hunts, one builds the shelter, and one cares for the young. Proving the power of reciprocity, Regan (1971) found that people were twice as likely to buy tombola tickets from a complete stranger if the stranger had shortly beforehand brought them a drink from the soda machine, and Strohmetz et al. (2002) found that diners tended to tip up to 26 percent more to waiters and waitresses who had left a couple of sweets with a personally addressed smile, with the check. So, before you start making requests and demands of your team, ask yourself: *what have I done for them?*

2. Scarcity: People want something more, if there is not much of it.

   In the months after Concorde announced it would be withdrawing its transatlantic service, bookings went through the roof with customers wanting to savor supersonic flight, while they still had the chance (Daily Mail, no date). The persuasive power of scarcity is why teleshopping channels show ever-decreasing purchase time-period countdowns, online stores highlight in red that there are only

X left of the product you are considering buying and airlines stress how few seats are left at your favored price. This principle supports the notion that not *only* expounding the benefits of any given challenge or project encourages uptake the most. To animate support for a proposal, also show your team member that this may be the last or at least a rare chance.

3. Authority: People tend to follow instructions from persons they feel hold a position of authority.

   Imagine that, while out in town for a walk, a person dressed in jeans and a sweater forbade you from entering a particular street, for no discernable reason. How would you feel? Now, picture the same situation, but the person blocking your way is wearing a security guard uniform or even a firefighter's hat. Would you react or feel differently? When we perceive the person talking to us to have authority, our respect for their suggestions and adherence to their instructions increases manifold.

   This has been shown to work in business. Cialdini (2012) mentions a real estate company that was able to increase the percentage of customer appointments by 20 percent and increase the percentage of contracts signed by 15 percent just by slightly changing the telephonist's patter. Instead of simply putting the caller through to the right specialist directly, switchboard operators were instructed to give a short, praiseworthy, glowing resumé of each real estate expert before they connected the caller. Callers exhibited greater respect for the real estate reps, not based on any KPIs (key performance indicators), USPs (unique selling propositions), or data that they had collected themselves, but merely based on apparent authority and expertise in people they had been told about. In a similar experiment, physios who hung diploma certificates on the wall were able to upsell their treatments considerably better than counterparts whose patients had not been informed of their qualifications, and so, authority. Perceived authority begins with rather banal manifestations such as a suitable outward appearance, punctuality, or honed social skills, but can be reinforced by a manager's reputation for professionalism and productivity. Perceived authority can be abused

(Milgram 1963), but in many cases, can help persuasion. Do you have authority in the eyes of your team?

4. Commitment: People like to be consistent in their decision making. Freedman and Fraser (1966) found that homeowners were far more likely to let supposed household product representatives into their house to inspect their detergents if the reps had already previously called on the phone to conduct a short survey on household products. In a similar experiment, Taylor and Booth-Butterfield (1993) found that, once house callers had won a metaphoric foot-in-the-door by convincing families to stick *drive carefully* stickers in their windows, they were twice as likely to agree to have a large, wooden *drive carefully* sign hammered into their front lawn. As a leader, try to keep your actions consistent and create fora where your team can express themselves regularly and routinely. When delegating tasks, keep the long game in mind.

5. Liking: People prefer to say yes to those whom they like.
Also known as the *halo effect* (Rosenzweig 2014), this principle suggests that, if we build up a relationship with our peers whereby they respect us and enjoy our company, they are far more likely to want to go the extra mile or jump through rings for us or indeed with us. Think about it. Would you prefer to help your dear friend repairing his or her garden fence or spend time helping that guy or girl down the road, whom you cannot stand, with his or her gardening? I am not suggesting that you develop false, pseudo-friendly relationships with people whom you do not like, but, if you have a reputation for being a polite, generous, hard-working, approachable executive, then you stand a far better likelihood of consensus and willingness from others to support. Studies have, repeatedly, bolstered this claim. One example, cited by Cialdini (2012) compared groups of MBA students in negotiations. One group was asked to employ a time-is-money approach to their talks, which came to agreements 55 percent of the time. The other group, who had been encouraged to get to know their negotiation partners before *getting down to business* came to agreement in 90 percent of cases. Nice guys do not always finish last!

6. Consensus: People observe decisions, made by others and tend to follow their lead.

In hotel bathrooms, you often find a card or sticker prodding you to pick up wet towels, and that in doing so, you will help to save the environment from polluting detergents. Both tidiness and environmental protection are, undoubtedly, commendable deeds, but research has shown that only about a third of hotel guests actually adhere to the USP-based suggestions on the bathroom notices. However, in one study, the rhetoric on the cards in hotel bathrooms was changed. The potential ecological advantages of hanging up towels was not mentioned. In its place, the announcement simply noted that the *majority* of people do not leave their towels on the floor. Strikingly, nearly twice as many guests choose to hang up their towels, just because *others apparently did so.* Conformity with peers is a strong human driver, as was shown by the infamous experiments by Dr. Asch (1951, 1952, 1956) (and since, by multiple replica studies, Bond and Smith 1996) and its implications should galvanize you to reflect on the culture that you would like to create or are creating in your team. More of this in Chapter 11.

Feedback

Imagine a colleague is about to go into an important meeting and is unsure as to whether he is dressed appropriately for the setting. He approaches you and asks you to give him some feedback on how he looks, what might your feedback sound like?

Maybe:

I like the shirt. The color suits you. You have got a tie on. The tie is red. Red is a sign of power. That waistcoat makes you look a bit like a waiter. I see you are wearing cufflinks. The cufflinks are a nice touch. If I am honest, I do not like the shoes you are wearing much and they do not go with the socks you have got on at all. Green and pink socks! Leather belt. Overall you look casual and smart, though.

Your colleague thanks you for the feedback and goes about his business. But, was that feedback?

I like the shirt, the color suits you, red is a sign of power, waistcoat makes you look like a waiter, cufflinks are a nice touch, I do not like the shoes, they do not go with the sock, casual, smart—all of these are not examples of feedback. They are opinions. Subjective, disputable, individual.

Green and pink socks, leather belt, tie on, tie is red, you are wearing cufflinks are also not examples of feedback. They are descriptive, objective, factual bits of information. There is no wiggle room here, no opinion.

The sentiment is not uncommon in the business world, but it is not feedback. Feedback is "goal-referenced; tangible and transparent; actionable; user-friendly specific and personalized; timely; ongoing; and consistent" (Wiggins 2012). The preceding comment on the colleague's dress and appearance is not feedback. It contains some of Wiggins' explication, but lacks a key ingredient. There is nothing in the preceding comment that helps the feedback receiver, moving forward. What Wiggins refers to as *actionable* is the essential ingredient in the perfect feedback cocktail. Without it, feedback is unusable, unhelpful, and cannot aid the recipient reflect and develop. A not-delicious cocktail.

Good feedback is invaluable to professional associates. Feedback is probably the most effectual communication tool at our disposal to develop our people and so help them to deliver best performance. Indeed, a large body of research into the way we learn has shown that providing feedback advances learning far better than teaching does (Bransford, Brown, and Cocking 2000; Hattie 2008; Marzano, Pickering, and Pollock 2001). However, despite its well-reported value, in my experience, feedback is one of the most neglected and poorly applied leadership techniques. Scores of executives I work with report a lack of feedback culture in their organizations or a culture of only giving negative, vindictive feedback. As Carole Robin from Stanford University notes (cited in Petersen 2013), feedback should be received and given gratefully and seen by both parties as a gift, an opportunity for improvement. It is certainly not a disciplinary tool nor should it be used as a deterrent.

Building on a model outlined by Hahnke (2017), my colleagues, Dr. Hans Werner Hagemann and Dr. Paul Schürmann, have developed a simple, concise formula for young leaders to deliver powerful, accurate, fair, and most importantly, developmental feedback.

The EECC Feedback Model (Hagemann 2018; Schürmann 2018)

Example: Explain the behavior that you observed. Try to describe only objective facts at this stage.

Effect: What effect did this behavior have on you? How did it make you feel? Be personal. Be subjective at this step to help the feedback receiver understand the reaction to their action.

Change: A suggestion as to how the feedback receiver can do things differently in the future. This is the key transformational step in effective feedback.

Or

Continue: A plea for the individual to forge ahead with their behavior and show more of it in the future.

Critical EECC feedback might sound like this:

I noticed that you arrived late for the client meeting, yesterday (example).

In my opinion, it left an unprofessional impression on our team, in front of the customers (effect).

I suggest you set yourself a reminder in the future, to ensure that you are on time. If you realize that you will not be punctual at the next meeting, please let us know beforehand (change).

Of course, EECC feedback works very powerfully, in much the same way, when given on positive accomplishments:

I saw the presentation you gave to the delegates on Thursday (example).

I loved the way you delivered it. It came across, for me, as punchy and entertaining (effect).

Keep up the good work. Use that entertaining style in your other presentations (continue).

A Few Final Tips on Giving Feedback

Practice. Developing your rhetoric in EECC feedback discourses might take some time, and your associates deserve to hear transformational feedback which is real world (example), lets them know what kind of impact their work has (effect), and helps develop them (change or continue). Good feedback is rarely spontaneous. Plan your words before you share them.

I-Message

When giving EECC feedback, if you can, start sentences with I or me instead of we, everyone, they, or one (Gordon 2008). The feedback is coming from you, and it should be very clear to the receiver that the effect has been made on you and not to imply that it has impacted anyone else. It is not for you to assume whom else their work might have affected. If others would also like to give feedback, then they are welcome to do so. This is your feedback, deliver it in I-message form.

Setting

Think about how you felt when your teacher told you off in front of the class or how you blushed, when your parents accused you of showing off in front of your visiting friends. Feedback should, where possible, be given privately. Consider any audience that might be in earshot, and what effect your feedback session might have on them or on the feedback receiver.

Timing

Try and get your feedback in as soon after the event as possible. Consider: Remember that presentation you gave nine months ago? Well, it was absolutely unacceptable. Buck up your ideas in future. Admittedly, the example is a bit extreme, but the timing of your feedback is hugely important in working toward transformational communication.

Active Listening

I have lost count of the amount of senior managers whom I have spoken to, who have chosen to name listening as their most valued leadership technique. We often organize so-called fireside chats, where junior managers have the opportunity to question senior executives on their career path and on their learnings from and philosophy on leadership. Invariably, sooner or later, the ubiquitous question comes up.

What would you say is the most important skill for a successful leader?

Nine times out of 10, the response is: listen. There is little argument that listening is a vital link in the communication chain (Bostrom and Bryant 1980), and yet, we spend time, money, and energy training our speaking and writing skills in workshops and online courses while we seldom develop our listening skills.

According to Dick Lee and Delmar Hatesohl from the University of Missouri (1993), we spend 70 to 80 percent of our waking hours communicating with only 45 percent of that time spent listening. Most of us communicate at around 125 words per minute, but we have the cognitive ability to listen to and understand anything up to 400 words per minute, and yet, sadly, we neglect this mental advantage of ours all too often.

As sociologist Les Back (2007) stated, ours is a culture of speaking not of listening. More and more, people feel the need to express themselves, share their opinions, make their presence known, and drop knowledge. In social media, reality TV shows, sports events, political rallies, the staff canteen, bars and cafés, meetings, open letters in the press ... we all seem to have something to say. But, how often do we genuinely stop to listen? According to sales guru Mark Wayshack (2014), listening "is entirely necessary in order to effectively understand what your prospects want, what they need and what they are looking to accomplish." He goes on to add that "You will sell far more effectively by doing most of the listening and only a little bit of the talking." While we are not focusing on sales in this book, I invite you to reflect on the notion that all of what we are doing as leaders involves persuasion and the selling of ideas and visions. (See Figure 9.1).

Listening should be your number one communication skill. Hone it. Wayshack (2014) recommends we spend 80 percent of our communication time listening and only the remaining 20 percent talking. Take a moment and recall how much of your leadership dialogue time, in the recent past, entailed you listening and how much involved others listening to you. Does your ratio come close to 80–20? Sadly, we do not only listen too little. We do not listen well-enough either. Research into listening has shown us that we forget around 50 percent of the information

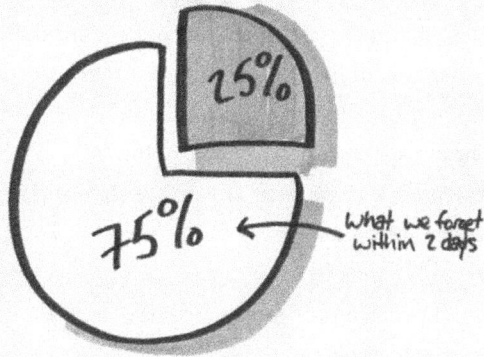

Figure 9.2 *Percentage of information we forget within 48 hours of hearing it*

just minutes after we have heard it, and a further 50 percent just 48 hours afterward. In other words, we commonly forget 75 percent of what we hear, no matter how it is delivered (Lee and Hatesohl 1993) (Figure 9.2). What adds insult to injury is that science has shown that our listening and retention skills get worse with age (Nichols 1957).

Without looking, can you recall all the statistics from the last paragraph? Can you name the scholars whose work gave us the data? What were those numbers again? Were you concentrating? Just a bit of fun, of course. But, it can be amazing and surprising how poor our information retention rate is.

What makes us such bad listeners? Ralph G. Nichols, the godfather of modern listening research, touted 10 typical listening bad habits in his talks and papers (cited in Lee and Hatesohl 1993), which we often slip into:

1. Call the subject matter uninteresting

    We go to a meeting or conference, noting the agenda items, having already convinced ourselves that what we are going to hear will be boring. As a result, what you hear (or do not hear) becomes a self-fulfilling prophecy.

2. Criticize the delivery or appearance of the speaker

   We often judge people (see Chapter 12, labeling) on their appearance, or personality traits, and let our assumptions about their character haze our ability to listen to what they have to say.

3. Become too stimulated

   We hear a speaker mention one point with which we disagree, and we then focus so intensely on that one point that we fail to capture following information.

4. Listen only for facts

   Some of us listen only for isolated data, and so miss the main points or themes of a speech.

5. Try to outline everything that is being said

   The opposite from bad habit 4. Some of us tend to try to organize and systematize in our minds, in real time, everything that we are hearing instead of trying to listen for gist.

6. Fake attention

   Oh, this one bugs me. The fake listener appears to be giving you his full attention, his eyes are on you, but his thoughts are elsewhere. The classic fake-attention-giveaway is the aha-royalty, who aha (agree) with what you are saying too often and often at illogical points.

7. Tolerate or create distractions

   Audience members who whisper or fiddle with their devices in meetings. It always makes me chuckle when my students at the university secretly tap on the cell phones, hidden under the desk. It is obvious to everybody what they are doing, but they raise their heads, post text message, with a smug look of accomplishment reminiscent of a spy who has just successfully tricked his mark.

8. Evade the difficult

   We tend to pick out the easily comprehensible parts of discourse and filter out the complex things.

9. Submit to emotional words

   We are suckers for emotive words. Republican, Democrat, northern, southern, black, white are examples of words that can often paint certain emotional pictures in the minds of listeners. Such language can be powerful, but it can also hinder information retention.

10. Waste thought power

Nichol's final bad listening habit is also his pet hate. He laments us wasting our talent for listening (400 words per minute) in favor of our speaking speed (125) words per minute. He has a point.

As Schilling (2012) puts it: "Genuine, listening has become a rare gift—the gift of time. It helps build relationships, solve problems, ensure understanding, resolve conflicts, and improve accuracy. At work, effective listening means fewer errors and less wasted time." That must be our goal at work, as leaders: to waste as little time as possible (re)dealing with misunderstandings, and instead use that time to be productive with the team.

The solution is active listening. Active listening originates from Carl Rogers and Richard Farson in 1957 and is the art of channeling focus and energy toward your interlocutor, in order to glean and retain as much information as possible, to aid the conversation flow, and to give your speaker the feeling, that he or she is being heard (which can bring about change in people) (Bodie et al. 2015). But, before we get down to the techniques, it is important to appreciate that they will not work, if you do not buy into the fundamental attitudes that underpin active listening. Our listening behavior will be "empty and sterile, and our associates will be quick to recognize this" (Rogers and Farson 1957). Put another way: this is not a method where you can fake it to make it. You first need to *want* to listen and understand before you can listen and understand.

Widely used in counseling, coaching, and therapy (Sharpe and Cowie 1998), active listening is an invaluable tool for the leadership toolbox, follow these active listening tips from Rogers and Farson to improve your transformational, leadership communication:

Listen for total meaning: What speakers say often comprises two components (known as speech acts): what they say actually (illocutionary act) and what they in fact want to convey (perlocutionary act) (Searle 1985). Do not be scared by the linguistics terminology here, what is important is that you differentiate between words and meaning. If your colleague says to you,
It is hot in here.

Her illocutionary act is to describe the temperature, but her perlocutionary act is possibly to share with you that she is uncomfortable in some way, that she would like you to open a window or take the meeting outside, and so on. What she says and means differ.

Respond to feelings: If a junior associate reports to you,

I have finished filing all the project documents.

You could confidently ascertain that he is ready for the next project. However, if the same associate had said,

I am so done with that godforsaken filing nonsense.

It is probably fair to say that he or she is not entirely emotionally connected with the task. You may want to think twice in future about assigning him or her such work.

In such active listening settings, try these communicative tricks. Reflecting: pick out the key messages and paraphrase them in your own, clear words back for your speaker. Summarizing: sum up the main points, including feelings that you are reading (Geldard and Geldard 1998).

Note All Cues

As we will take a deeper look at in the next chapter, not all communication is verbal, so keep an eye out for other communication channels used by your speaker. How is he or she inflecting his or her speech, what is the facial expression as he or she talks, how is he or she sitting or standing, that is, what nonverbal cues are being sent? Eye movement, breathing, hand gestures, fiddles, and other physical cues also all help to convey the complete speech act. Transformational, active listening involves (as strongly suggested in its name) that you, the listener, get active. The leader who waves his associate in, exclaiming, Come in. I am listening, without once looking up from his computer screen is not actively listening. Get active. Lean into the discussion, listen and look out for all cues, paraphrase and comment (do not repeat like a parrot or *aha* ad nauseum) and endeavor to understand, not just to hear. Your associates deserve your attention, and you might just learn something.

Chapter Leadership Challenge

The three Ps: practice, practice, practice.

Try and find as many opportunities as possible to train your communication skills. Ask everyone you know, if you may offer them some feedback and use the EECC format. If you are worried about a backlash at first, feel free to start with giving positive EECC feedback before moving on to more challenging critical feedback. The more you practice the format, the more natural it will become until you will instinctively give EECC feedback whenever asked.

The same goes for active listening. Start with friends or family. Ask someone to tell their story and *just listen*. Do not focus on your performance, focus on what you hear, feel, notice, and glean from the talk. Give your speaking partner EECC feedback on *what* they told you and on *how* they came across as they delivered their speech.

CHAPTER 10

Talk the Talk

Too Many Leaders Just Do Not Know How to Communicate Right

The Sharpest Tool in the Box

As a management trainer, one has to travel a lot, and only just recently, I climbed into a taxi at Frankfurt airport and asked the driver to take me to the hotel where I was to be delivering a leadership workshop for the next three days. Now, some taxi drivers leave you to yourself in the back seat. They concentrate on the road and the route, and you do not hear much else out of them other than the ubiquitous "where to?" at the beginning and the concise "do you need a receipt?" toward the end of the trip. Some taxi drivers, on the other hand, just *love* to talk. On this particular day, I had snagged a chatty *cabby* (as they call them in London). He seemed to want to squeeze in anecdotes of every interesting passenger he had ever had sit in his car together with asking me to regale him of my life story, all in the paltry 12 minutes we shared together.

Upon discovering what I do as my profession, he duly asked me *the question*. The question, which, in my experience, is the one single question I have had to answer the most, in my career:

"So, what is the most important thing you need, to make you a good manager?," my taxi driver enquired.

I gave my friendly driver that day the same answer I will give you here. After having worked with tens of thousands of leaders and leaders-in-the-making in my career and deconstructed their skills, strengths, and weaknesses together with them, in my opinion, the single most important tool for a leader is: communication.

If you cannot communicate, you cannot delegate.

If you cannot communicate, you cannot work strengths-oriented.

If you cannot communicate, you cannot motivate.

If you cannot communicate, you cannot inspire....

And, the list goes on and on. Of all the gifts granted to us by the magic of evolution, no other separates us from our animal cousins more than our ability for detailed, applied, subjective, and objective communication, be it ad hoc or planned. What is more, we all seem to know just how important communication is, and yet time and time again, I am surprised to hear of leaders who struggle to have found their voices. I regularly hear incandescence, gratitude, shock, or amazement (or sometimes all of these) from leader coaches of mine who—after having asked my advice on how they should deal with this conflict or that staff appraisal, with this unmotivated associate or that unfocused team member—hear my response:

"Have you spoken to the person(s) concerned about that, yet?," I invariably ask.

"Oh, what a good idea!"

"No, not yet, I was meaning to get around to it."

"No, but I will definitely arrange to do so, right away."

"No. I didn't know what to say." Coachees inevitably respond.

It astonishes me how *few* young leaders reach for candid, open, transparent communication when faced with leadership challenges. In one executive coaching session on the phone recently, the coach from a global player tool manufacturer; Matt from Australia, fell silent when I asked him if he had yet spoken to the parties involved. There was no answer. After several seconds of nothing, I feared we had been cut off and so asked: "Matt, are you still there?" "Yes!," he replied immediately. "You can hear me thinking!"

Matt, like so many, had not thought of communicating with his associates to address his issue or he at least had not yet developed the appropriate arguments or created the right setting. In this chapter, I would like to take you on a crash course of communication fundamentals, and hope there is something there that will give you the tools to find the right words for your team in the future.

What You Say

Think of a tree.

Go on. Think of a tree. Build a picture of it in your head and save that picture.

Ok. What does your tree look like? Does it have a full, green crown, and does fruit hang from its branches? Or, is it maybe a tree in winter, all its leaves shed, standing tall and strong, but with no greenery? Can you maybe see its roots? Or is it a different shape altogether? A palm, Christmas, or even family tree?

If we asked everyone currently reading this book to draw the trees, chances are we would have a variety of different trees. Indeed, I often ask participants to sketch their trees, and we get the works; all types of different tree manifestations. Carl Wieman (2007) refers to this as "the curse of knowledge" and describes it as "the idea that when you know something, it is extremely difficult to think about it from the perspective of someone who does not know it" (2007). A classic laboratory example of this is the 1990 study by Elisabeth Newton, which showed that only one out of 40 listeners could identify a song being tapped out onto a table, but that those doing the tapping had predicted that half would be able to name the tune. We often forget that our audience does not share our knowledge. The curse of knowledge is apparent when we give our colleagues instructions and are confused, when they do not fulfill them to your expectations.

Why did I ask you to think of a tree, and why should we care that there are multiple renditions of the word, or that some people cannot identify tapped songs, as well as the tapper expects? Because it is important for us as considered communicators to appreciate that even the simplest of words or concepts in our mind (for example *tree*) can construe different images in the heads of different interlocutors. Just because we, as the speaker, know what we mean or expect, when we say a word, does not mean that our listeners will immediately have the same *picture* in their minds. Why should they? They may not know what I know.

As a leader, choose your words very carefully. Choose them not based on whether you feel they may be the new buzz words, sound impressive or for any other reason. Choose your words in such a way that your audience will best understand.

When we find our vocabulary, what to say? The Heath brothers in their book on catchy communication: *Make it Stick* (2008) classify three simple yet powerful ways of making what we say, stick in the minds of those listening to us.

1. Make it mysterious. I call this the Batman effect. Remember the cliff-hangers at the end of each episode of the Batman series in the 1960s? (Created by Lorenzo Semple Jr.). Batman was trapped, strapped to a bench while the Joker aimed a laser between his legs. Frustratingly, we had to wait in those days for a week to find out, whether Batman lived or died. Invariably, Robin would save Batman, but our attention was held and the narrative stuck (even for seven days between shows).
2. Make it unexpected. Ask yourself: *What is my audience expecting to hear?* Can I offer them something unexpected that they will not forget in a hurry?
3. Make it personal. Generic language flies over us like a migrating bird on its way to more clement weather. We barely notice it go. We pay it only the briefest of attention and then think nothing more of it until we see birds returning months later. Keep your language specific and individualized. Involve your listener and stress how things affect him or her.

Red-hot trends in communication inhibition in recent years include:

- The use of business buzzwords;
- Borrowing words from other vocabularies; and
- My personal favorite communication hindrance: the acronym.

Liz Ryan (2018) at Forbes magazine notes her 10 most cringe-worthy buzzwords of 2018:

1. Paradigm (or paradigm shift)
2. At the end of the day
3. Deliverables
4. Core competency

5. Best practice

6. Deep dive or drill down or 10,000-foot view

7. Synergy

8. Game-changer or disrupter

9. Blue-sky thinking

10. Right-sizing

Do you find yourself using words like these or similar jargon or phraseology? If so, I would like to invite you to reflect on how sure you are that your discourse partner understands. I am not telling you to banish such words from your vocabulary; metaphoric language can be very powerful and productive. I am suggesting you consider the chances that such words might be misconstrued, when even the word *tree* can paint a hundred mental pictures.

Translation blogger Manny Echevarria (2008) cites some common loanwords, pawned from other tongues, regularly heard in English, including:

Schadenfreude
[German] The pleasure one takes from someone else's misfortune.

Modus operandi
[Latin] Someone's habits or method of operating (often used by police investigators to describe someone's criminal profile, or MO)

Faux pas
[French] The violation of a commonly accepted social rule, a blunder like a gaffe.

Aficionado
[Spanish] An ardent admirer or fan of something.

Doppelgänger
[German] A double, or look-alike person, often with negative connotations because some people believe that seeing your own doppelgänger is an omen of impending death.

L'enfant terrible
[French] A child who says or does really embarrassing things, or a successful adult whose achievements were executed in an unorthodox way.

Prima donna
[Italian] Literally, *first lady* as in the principal female singer in an opera, but usually used to refer to a spoiled, ill-tempered person.

Mea culpa
[Latin] Literally, *my own fault.* Usually used by a person who is admitting guilt for some wrong-doing.

Quid pro quo
[Latin] Literally, *something for something.* Often used in place of *you scratch my back and I will scratch yours* or during negotiations to ask, *what is in it for me?*

Zeitgeist
[German] The spirit of the times. Used to describe things in the socio-cultural air, like trends or ideas that describe an era.

How many of those do you know or use?

Once again, my message here is not to eliminate loanwords from your arsenal or that they are bad in any way. Language changes (Betz 1959). A language's lexicon (the words at its speakers' disposal) grows, swells, moves, develops. Words are lost, and words are assimilated all the time (Vilar 2007). And, that is fine. My only invitation to you is to have a long hard think about whether or not the word or words that you have chosen to borrow to make your point, actually ended up being faux amis, because your speaking partner does not follow your leitmotiv.

And finally, in this section: my pet bugbear: the acronym. The character Chandler from the hugely successful 1990's comedy series F•R•I•E•N•D•S had a job, which his buddies did not understand. As part of his dull, on-the-job duties, he and his work colleagues referred to office concepts with funny acronyms: "wenus" (weekly estimated net usage systems), and "ANUS" (annual net usage statistics) (Myerson 1995). These play-on-word business acronyms have, of course, been created for comic effect by the series' creators, but just about every company that I have worked together with over the years has used its own industry acronyms, corporation acronyms and some even use their own departmental or team-specific abbreviations. My issues with this are twofold.

1. Acronyms can, potentially, stand for distinct concepts and carry multiple connotations (compare: South Lake Union Trolley and the Wisconsin Tourism Federation) and
2. Newer members of teams often have not yet added such acronyms to their vocabulary, and so are being left behind by their usage.

Educate your team. Provide glossaries. Be transparent and choose your words very, very carefully.

How You Say It

Now, compare the following sentences:

> *It* does not matter that you did that.
> It *does not* matter that you did that.
> It does not *matter* that you did that.
> It doesn't matter *that* you did that.
> It doesn't matter that *you* did that.
> It doesn't matter that you *did* that.
> It doesn't matter that you did *that*.

When the word in *italics* is stressed the most, the seeming synonymous sentences take on distinct meanings. Here we can see the importance not only of *what* one says but also *how* one says it. The emphasis on words can change the implied or inferred missive, but to the same extent, the manner with which I communicate also affects how my message arrives at the receiver (Shannon and Weaver 1949; Schramm 1954). Volume, timbre, body posture, gesticulation facial mimic, and even our frame of mind can dramatically influence how what we say comes across.

With regards to body language, there are a lot of great treatise out there, and I would recommend Ekman et al.'s (1987) work on reading facial micro expressions as a useful leadership tool to add to your stock, but unfortunately both would be too much for the scope of this book. Suffice to say that *how* I say something is often more important than *what* I veritably say. It is for this reason that call-center telephonists are trained to smile as they answer the phone. The smile, even on the unseen speaker's face, positively affects how their communication on the phone comes across.

An exemplary case of the *how* in communication topping the what is when then President Kennedy stood in front of the Brandenburg Town Hall in West Germany in 1963 and erroneously declared to the over 400,000 stood in the square, listening: "ich bin ein Berliner!" (Provan 2013). Those words have gone down in history as one of the great speeches on the subject of freedom, and the crowd that day cheered excitedly to Kennedy's words, but what he actually said was grammatically incorrect and carries a very different meaning in German. (Daum 2008). "Ich bin Berliner" would have meant "I am a Berlin native" or "I am one of you" (surely his intention), but unfortunately "Ich bin *ein* Berliner" actually means "I am a donut" (the Berliner is a type of butter donut, often filled with jam). What is noteworthy is that neither the predominantly German-speaking audience that day, nor most watching at home, noticed Kennedy's slip. The attractive man with an existing, strong reputation for public speaking, the huge flag fluttering behind him, the impeccable suit he had on with his perfectly bound tie, the careful gesticulation, the way he held his head high and annunciated his words clearly, and with purpose was what the audience actually recorded. According to Mehrabian (1967, 1967b), only 7 percent of the message and personal feelings I send to you originate from the words that come out of my mouth. The tone of my voice (38 percent) and my body language (55 percent) account for the vast majority of influence on you as to how much you will like what I say.

For the Toolbox

Hands up. Who has taken part in a meeting that resembled any of the following descriptions.

- Boring
- Unfocused, there seems to be little connection between statements

- A waste of time
- Just a chance for people to make their case or defend their agenda
- Not relevant for me. Why was I invited?
- People talking over each other
- Too long
- People are getting distracted, sidetracked

And, what format did the vast majority of those meetings take? Probably, a small group of invited people, sitting around a table, talking. There is probably or maybe an agenda, minutes are often taken by someone or other, and the meeting is usually chaired by someone, but discussion bounces back and forth, and all the phenomena listed may occur.

It does not have to be that way, all the time. If you are *driving the bus*, if it is your meeting, then why not try out some different ways of communicating? Here is a selection of a few communication tools to help improve your transformational communication:

Talking Stick

One of the oldest communication tools. Our forefathers realized too that communication can sometimes lose focus, and so, many people when meeting with tribe or group members would use a simple stick, stone, or other object to try to control communication flow. The rule is simple: whoever is holding the talking stick talks, whoever is not holding it listens. It is incredible how powerful such a simple tool can be. People really do listen and it hones speakers' rhetoric too, so we get productivity on both sides. The stick-holder, when finished, can then invite someone else to talk by offering him or her the stick or others can express their desire to talk next with a simple open hand gesture (asking for the stick) or with a nod or with eye contact.

Poker Chips

A variation on the talking stick is to work with poker chips, matchsticks, coins, or something similarly small and collectable. If you feel that discussion in a particular meeting could slip off point, then assign each meeting attendee with, say, three chips, and inform them that each time they would like to contribute (for example 45 seconds per speech), they will have to *pay* with one of their chips. In this case, each person would be limited to three inputs. This comms tool focuses people's thoughts and trains them to keep to their point. Such structure can help meetings to be much more productive.

Peer Consultation

This communication setting originates from the social sciences, but is popping up in a business context more and more. It works particularly well for meeting participants, who have a specific challenge or problem and would like input and opinion from their peers to hopefully help them consider new alternatives to a given professional situation. It works perfectly with 5- to 8-person groups. Get the group together and then invite anyone or everyone to suggest cases that they would like to discuss. Explanations should be short. Two to three minutes max. The group then chooses one case (others can be discussed at later sessions), and the peer consultation begins.

Five minutes: The case bringer explains her situation and poses one specific question to the group that she would like help with.

10 minutes: The group asks concept-checking questions of the case bringer to assure comprehension. *Mrs. X you talk about - how long has she been working here? The product you mention, is it on budget? The colleague you are in a conflict with - how well do you know them?'* and so on.

20 minutes: The case bringer turns her chair round 180 degrees (so that she has her back to the group). She takes a pen and paper to take notes, but takes *no* part in this *part* of the consultation. The rest of the group talk about or her and the case as if she was not there. *I think she should do the following..., I feel that her mistake was when she...,* and so on.

Five minutes: Feedback. The case bringer turns back to the group, thanks them for their engagement, and feeds back on what she has heard. Maybe some of the suggestions or ideas were new, maybe she has tried or considered some before. Either way, she shares that with the group, show-ing that she might have gotten some new impulses (positive) or received confirmation that the already tried tactics were recommended (positive).

Interestingly, with this setting, the participants do not necessarily have to know or understand the case bringer's industry or field. Sometimes, a lay brainstorm can stray out-of-the-box and inspire new thought and reflection. Some people like to try this setting with the case bringer leaving the room altogether for the 20-minute discussion period. This might add a greater level of freedom of expression to the peers, but summary and convergence of findings might be more effortful. Try both and see which one works for you and your team.

6 Hats

De Bono (2017) suggests six ways in which the brain can be challenged to judge a situation through a different perspective, and so release potentially different cognitive thought. In this brainstorming setting, each of the six directions is represented by a certain colored *hat*. When metaphorically *wearing* each hat, the speaker should be inspired to think about the issue at hand only as that type of character would think. The hats represent the following thought classes:

Blue: The manager, facilitator, moderator. Sticking to the goal, sticking to the subject, sees the big picture.

White: The wearer of the white hat focuses only on numbers, data, facts, and objective information.

Red: Emotions and instinctive gut reactions, but without loading the statements with any kind of judgment.

Black: The cautious, practical hat. Exercises realism and expresses conservative prudence.

Yellow: Optimism. Sees the potential bright side of situations and uses logic to sniff out harmony and accord.

Green: Provocative, out-of-the-box, creative thinking. Takes an idea and runs with it in a flow of inventive consciousness.

Individuals and organizations have used the brainstorm tool for years in order to attempt to approach an issue from multiple angles, to explore myriad options. A communicative, team variation of this process is to designate each member of a six-strong team a *hat* (either metaphorically or literally), and then review a matter together, with each hat owner only contributing in the assigned manner to which his or her hat allows, that is, the red hat wearer only comments with shoot-from-the-hip emotion, while the one with the yellow hat only makes positive contributions.

Simulations

Simulations can be particularly helpful for empowering team members to have confidence to deal with high-pressure communication situations such as sales pitches, negotiations, interviews, staff appraisals, and so forth. Days before the real-world discourse at hand is due to take place, arrange for those involved to gather with some volunteers to simulate or role-play the talk. Give heaps of feedback after each role play and do not be afraid to press the *pause* button, give immediate, specific input on a particular turn of phrase, then *rewind* the talk and have the speaker instantaneously practice the new suggestion. Experiment with using video cameras to allow for the speaker to appreciate how they are perceived by others, and if you get the chance, try working with professional seminar actors who can ingeniously reproduce speaker styles, based on just a few bits of information about the character they are portraying.

Fishbowl

Better for larger groups, the bowl setting can bring fluidity into a communication environment, where, without it, chaos or stagnation could ensue. In the fishbowl, a handful of speakers are chosen (perhaps based on their expert knowledge of a particular issue) or volunteer to join the moderator in a small, inner circle of chairs. The rest of the attendees close a larger circle of chairs around the smaller circle, enclosing them like fish in a fishbowl. The size of the whole fishbowl can be anything from 15 to 20 people up to hundreds (the largest fishbowl I have been involved in had 20 podium speakers in the middle and 350 in concentric outer circles), and the dynamism comes from the size.

It is highly recommended that a fishbowl has a content-neutral chair or facilitator whose job is to steer the discussion from item to item with well-timed questions aimed at always-changing podium speakers. But, the real magic begins when members of the outer circles decide to contribute. Unlike podium discussions, where the speakers remain the same, fishbowl outer-circle members can stand, enter the inner circle, tap any inner-circle speaker on the shoulder, and then take their place in the inner circle and immediately begin augmenting the discussion. This fluency brings fresh input and arguments to a discussion while allowing an audience to remain large. Without the swapping proffered by the fishbowl, large groups could suffer from chaotic noise and cross-speaking or be impaired by only a few, blinkered views. The fishbowl provides an alternative to both these disadvantages.

Chapter Leadership Challenge

Next time you have to chair a meeting, try one of the settings. Be transparent with your team and tell them if you find some of the meetings stagnant, and that you would like to try some different settings to try to improve productivity. Get some feedback (ask for it in the EECC format) on how your colleagues found the methods.

Before the next big presentation or discourse, take a few minutes to plan what you would like to say and how you would like to say it. Put thought into what order you would like to deliver the information, with what levels of pathos, ethos, and logos and packaged with what kind of body language. When I first started work, I would make myself little notes to remind me to stand for this argument, sit for that, lean forward at that moment, and so on. Preplanning the delivery method can help you to develop a more natural and convincing communication style.

CHAPTER 11

Company Culture

Culture Is Not Only a Nation-to-Nation Thing

The Trunk of the Tree

I once asked a group of young potentials to produce their image of a perfect leader. The vision they conceived was of a tree. It was not the first time that I had heard leadership (or other abstract constructs, for that matter) described using the metaphor of a tree (Figure 11.1). But, it was the first time that I had seen it expressed in quite this way. The group posited one's *kitchen table* values (see Chapter 2) as the roots on which any healthy leader-tree feeds, in order to grow and the leaves, branches, blossom, and fruits represented the output or tangible or perceivable leadership style. Nice. I got the analogy, but, in all honesty, it had not bowled me over reflectively, up to that point. But, the way they presented the trunk caught my eye. This group envisaged the trunk of the tree; the stable structure that supports the whole crown; the mast that—when diseased—poisons everything above and below it; the torso of the frame that, if cut down, suffocates all growth as *organizational culture*. This metaphor I like.

No matter how transformational leaders act, irrespective of how unshakably they identify with their values and inner beliefs, the culture of communication and work ethic around them can irrevocably affect their ability to lead as they would like. The internal culture of each organization of people is distinct, and each has developed its own nuanced approach to problem-solving, communication channels and direction, respect of hierarchy and subordination, not to mention the makeup of different bodies, processes, and structures each company and organization has

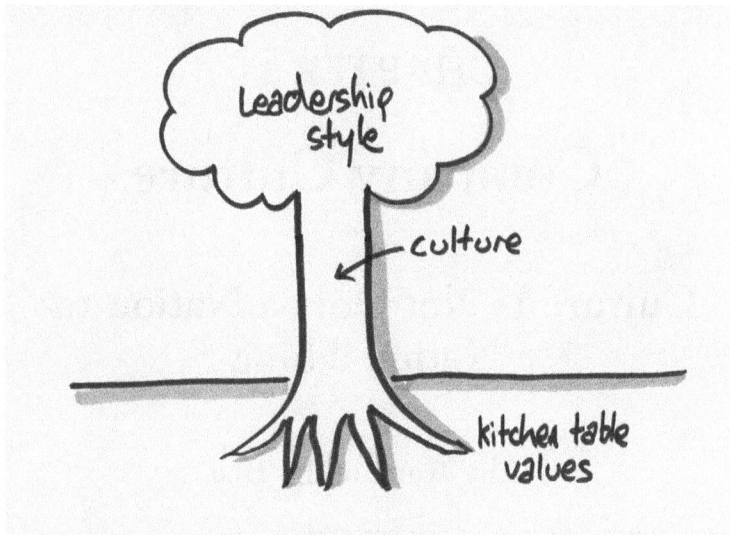

Figure 11.1 Culture is the trunk of the leadership tree

established. Peter Drucker is famously credited (Cave 2017)[1] with having said: "culture eats strategy for breakfast." What Drucker is suggesting here is that ignorance to the (existing) power of a culture of a team or unit is to open yourself up for potential failure as a leader, no matter where your motivations lie or how detailed your planning is.

Continuing the metaphor[2], what is of interest is that the trunk of the tree affects both what is above it and below it, both positively and negatively. If the trunk is healthy and strong, then the crown of the tree will blossom and thrive. By the same token, if the trunk is unhealthy, then it can contaminate both its own root system and the surrounding soil. The culture of the plant affects its surroundings. In the botanical world, the lupin flower gives off nitrogen into the earth around it, and oak trees release tannic acid. In other words, our culture and establishment impacts everything around it—our values, our processes and output, and the climate we perform in. Culture can be very cogent, in all directions.

---

[1] It has often been disputed as to whether Drucker actually said this (Anders 2016; Cave 2017).

[2] I am grateful to Doreen Köhler for this analogy.

We usually hear the word culture with regards to describing national tendencies or stereotypical traits of people in different countries. But, culture can establish itself and affect the interaction and actions of any sized group from just a handful of people up to networks of millions. Indeed, intercultural guru Geert Hofstede describes culture as "The collective programming of the mind that distinguishes the members of one category of people from another" (1991). This somewhat provocative use of the word *programming* implies trance-like, robotic response from group members, but programming is exactly what happens, when we slowly, but surely learn and observe each other's behavior and develop similar attitudes in order to comply and feel comfortable within that group. Such patterned responses are deeply rooted in our limbic survival instincts (see Chapter 7) and our forefathers' and mothers' desires to congregate in tribes to share responsibilities in a strengths-oriented manner and to search for safety in numbers from predators (Harari 2014). Developing similar traits to counterparts over time is absolutely human and very natural.

Hofstede conducted a huge quantitative, anthropomorphic study in the 1960s and 1970s interviewing 118,000 people from 40 different countries (this dataset was later added to by other scholars to encompass responses from over 90 nationalities) and established a six-dimensional[3] cultural model. According to Hofstede, different groups cope with

1. Inequality (Hofstede calls this power distance index, PDI),
2. Uncertainty (uncertainty avoidance index, UAI),
3. Relationship with(in) the group (individualism versus collectivism, IDV),
4. Masculine and feminine attitudes (MAS),
5. Long-term orientation (LTO), and
6. Indulgence (indulgence versus restraint, IND)

to lesser or greater amounts. Although Hofstede's dimensions have been used for decades to compare national groups, their precepts can be

---

[3] Initially, Hofstede composed four cultural dimensions, but these were expanded to six after work from Micheal Bond (1991) and Micheal Minkov (2010).

used to help leaders observe cultural traits in organizational cultures in equal measure.

PDI deals with the concept of how subordinates and superiors interact and respect each other's authority. Do members of staff question or openly challenge decisions made by superiors or do they subserviently accept instructions, irrespective of whether they agree with them or not. In groups with high PDI, subordinates accept paternalistic or autocratic decisions, and superiority is taken for granted. Hierarchy is rigid and abiding. In low PDI cultures, hierarchies are flatter and decision-making channels free of dictum.

Cultures with high IDV are ones where the individuals' focus is on personal achievements, whereby members of the collectivist groups act as part of a whole and prioritize group interests and goals ahead of their own achievements and recognition.

How groups deal with ambiguity and uncertainty is UAI. Organizations with lots of rules, regulations, and resistance to change differ strongly from teams where decision making is more agile, team members are open-minded to change, new direction or risk and the culture is one of openness to new concepts and strategies.

According to Hofstede, networks of people with strong MAS exhibit traits such as: competitiveness, assertiveness, materialism, ambition, power. Groups that he describes as feminine more typically value relationships, quality of life, and respect over more obvious materialistic gains.

A subculture's time horizon is illustrated with LTO. If a group focuses on the future, is long term in its planning and strategic approach, is persistent and pragmatic when achieving goals oriented toward success and reward, then it is a high LTO group. Other cultures may show evidence of focusing more on past achievements, aggrandizing tradition, and holding face-saving as more important than direct, transparent communication. Teams with low LTO reciprocate deeds, as a sign of respect for former acts.

IND cultures allow for fun and indulgence and encourage freedom of expression and celebration. Success is often openly celebrated and lines of business and pleasure are more blurred. Team-building measures may proliferate, and the team celebrates together. Some teams show more restraint and suppress gratification. Open celebration may be considered unfocused or unprofessional, and more importance is given to moving on to the next project and not *wasting* time and money on celebrating perceived successes.

Keep an eye out for your organization's culture. Does the whole corporation exude the same cultural traits or do different divisions manifest Hofstede's dimensions to differing amounts? If you are new to the group, enquire about its culture and ask colleagues for tips on what cultural strategies they used to assimilate into the group. Can you see any parts of your group's cultural tree that you think might be poisoning the soil or the branches? What decisions would you make as a leader, if any, to change the culture in your team?

The mix of how much or how little of each of the culture dimensions any group may exhibit gives us the culture apparent in our organization. According to Schürmann (2018) there are six typical organizational cultures:

Power culture: Fear, public rewards and penalties, change driven from senior management, strategy is driven by one personality, checks and balances follow our every move in this culture.

Team culture: Self-accountability, feeling of *we* as opposed to *them and us*, collaboration proliferates, and team members motivate one another to follow shared goals. Strong levels of accepted individuality.

Consensus culture: The individuals bow to the groups' perceived wishes and needs. There is a lack of individuality and personality. Conflicts are avoided and compromises preferred. Hierarchy does not inhibit performance.

Patriarchal culture: Dominant behavior patterns abound, senior members of staff are respected, and the leadership style is very personality-driven. Loyalties are hugely important and love or respect must be earned and can be easily lost. That image originates from the father or mother figure at the head of the organization. Usually, no succession planning and lesser chances of employee movement. Common in family-run organizations.

Bureaucratic culture: Unnecessary levels of regulations and rules. The amount of and complexity of processes stifles productivity and creativity. Employees are required to follow a set path to promotion. Such cultures are very self-involved, emotions and personal opinions are hidden, and the buck is regularly passed.

Hierarchical culture: Junior management defers by default to more senior executives. Control is exerted with the use of privileges (company cars, parking spaces, business class travel, corner offices, and so on). Information is shared selectively, and discipline is expected and punished when broken. Ranks and responsibilities are well known.

Whichever culture is prevalent in your organization, the vital point to keep in mind is how strongly culture can drain or encourage productivity. Culture is the third cog in the business wheel, without which the machine will not turn and which sets your corporation apart from the rest (be it for better or worse). As you can see in the following diagram (Hagemann 2018), the structure of an organization tends to be rigid (Figure 11.2). Add to that the (often top-down) set strategy, and it is no surprise that many traditional, large companies are finding things increasingly difficult in this modern, volatile, uncertain, complex, and ambiguous (VUCA) (Bennett and Lemoine 2014) world we live in today. In recent generations, such (infra)structure and long-term strategy (including set, established supplier, and supply chains) served corporations well as they tried to keep production costs low through economies of scale and provide for their (usually) stable market and their well-known, recognizable, usually faithful target

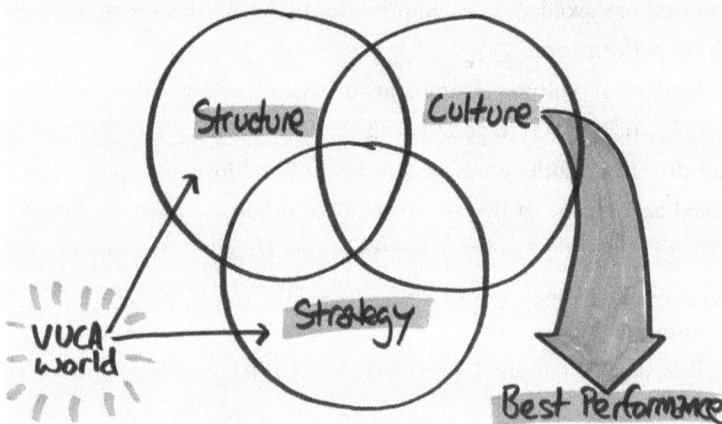

Figure 11.2 Only agile organizational culture can produce best performance in a VUCA world

group. But today, in our VUCA world (Hagemann 2018), where the largest real estate company in the world (airbnb) does not own any property, where the most successful taxi company in the world (uber) does not own any vehicles, and where products and services are produced for markets, which hitherto did not exist; for target groups, who did not know that they wanted the things in the first place (see tablets, apps, wearables, and so on)—all bets are off. Structure and strategy have been our friends in the business world in the past, but moving forward, agility through culture will make or break every organization born in the 21st century.

It is only with the development of a flexible, strengths-oriented, winning culture, combined with lean processes and talent that we will release the potential in future teams and facilitate leaders to add value in the next decades.

With the power of culture established, where does this culture thing come from, anyway?

The Monkey Paradigm

Once upon a time, there was a zoo and there were five monkeys in the monkey enclosure. One day, the zookeeper decided to try out an experiment. She placed a bunch of bananas on the floor near the monkeys and took a step back. Then, as the first monkey approached the bananas, she grabbed a hose and sprayed the monkey that had tried to help itself to the banana bounty *and* all the other four monkeys. The lead monkey returned, disgruntled to his friends. All were soaking. All were very sad.

The next day the zookeeper positioned some bananas again and this time something different happened. As the second monkey approached the bananas, the others, not wanting to get drenched by the zookeeper's hose, beat him black and blue. The monkey changed his mind and did not try for the bananas. The beating had persuaded him otherwise. On the third day, a third monkey tried for the bananas, and she too was prevented from doing so by a beating from her monkey colleagues, none of whom wanted to get sprayed. On the fourth day, the fourth monkey was bashed for approaching the bananas, and the same happened to the fifth monkey on day five. All knew: if you go for the bananas, we all get wet, so anyone trying, will be whacked.

One day, the first monkey was transferred to another zoo, and soon afterward, a new monkey arrived. Upon seeing the bananas, he immediately ventured toward them only to get summarily beaten up. Not understanding what had happened, he slouched off into a corner. One day, all four of the remaining original monkeys had been transferred to other zoos and had been replaced with other monkeys. On that day, there are five new monkeys in the enclosure, none of whom has ever been sprayed for stealing bananas. The next day the fifth new monkey sees the loot, goes for the fruits and is duly scratched, thrashed, and punished by the other apes. With consternation, he loafs back toward the pen and (presumably in monkey-language) asks: why did you all beat me up when I went for the bananas?

And they all, in unison, respond,

We do not know why we beat you up when you motioned toward the bananas—*it is what we have always done!*

That is how a culture paradigm establishes itself and how a culture of behavior develops. Often blindly, often inadvertently, and usually slowly. In a similar vein to how a mother only notices the growth of her child when a shocked relative arrives at the door and cries in consternation at the sight of the nephew,

Wow, how you have grown!

So too can culture creep up on a group. Mr. Twit in Roald Dahl's grim and ghoulish children's book *The Twits* (Dahl 2003), wanting to prank his pesky wife, adds a slither of wood to the bottom of her walking stick every day for weeks until one day Mrs. Twit notices that walking with her stick has become difficult, and she comes to the only logical conclusion: that she is shrinking. The unnoticed drip-by-drip lengthening has driven her to perceive the problematic status quo all wrong. We do not observe culture developing, but we oh-so-often complain about and suffer under its ramifications after it has established itself as normal in our surroundings.

As a leader, you have a powerful opportunity to drive the culture in your team toward strengths orientation (see Chapter 4), reward mode (Chapter 7), and productivity, but you first have a responsibility to appreciate what is making your walking stick lengthen and then to ask yourself: what kind of culture would I like to work in? When you have the answer, your first responsibility to live by those values (see Chapter 1) every next day.

Role Model

My trainer colleague and project management maestro Christine Ait-Mokhtar once regaled me of the following story about a former leader she knew.

The boss, a medical doctor, was described as a workaholic, high-intensity manager, who set herself extremely high standards and openly expected equally high-level performance from her team. Part of the boss's demands was that her staff's attendance be as exemplary as hers. Thought-provokingly, the boss, to ensure that she was never absent from work, self-prescribed herself with the medicine she felt she needed to keep her on her feet and working to the optimum. Of course, her team did not have such ready access to prescription drugs to keep them work-ready. Resultantly, an unfortunate subculture developed within the team due to the combination of the boss's famously high attendance expectations twinned with her penchant to self-medicate. Namely, the team, unable to write themselves prescriptions to keep giving themselves the boost needed to attend work, started attending work despite illness, for fear of castigation from their superior. A culture of staff coming to work although sick developed and the negatives for staff health, patient health, staff welfare, team motivation, and of course, productivity or efficiency are obvious.

As leaders, we carry a huge responsibility to act as role models. Setting high expectations of your team is fine, but are the expectations realistic? Are your well-intentioned standards creating a culture of expectation management which is unfair, unethical, or unrealistic? Team members might either look up to their leaders to watch, learn, and copy, or they might observe your questionable behavior and expect to be able to act in a similar manner. Subordinates invariably follow their leader's lead (for better or worse). If I am late, does that mean it is okay for my subordinates to be late? Do my emotional outbursts at work give others the green light to shout and scream? Does my corner-cutting infect my team and lead to a culture of *that will do*? Return to your standards we discussed in Chapter 1 and assess what kind of role model you would like to be and what kind of culture you intend to establish in your department.

Research has shown that "self-enhancement values related positively to charismatic leadership, which predicted managerial performance and followers' extra effort" (Sosik 2005).

According to leadership expert Martin Webster (2018), there are six core elements to becoming a transformational leader role model:

1. Be motivated. You cannot motivate others if you are not motivated yourself.
2. Self-reflection. Self-reflective leaders strive to constantly self-develop and set high standards for themselves and their team.
3. Self-awareness. Be open to new ideas and never stop learning.
4. Empathy. When you are aware of your own impact, you will genuinely impact on others.
5. Vision, courage, and integrity. If you do not have a clear vision of where you are going, why should anyone follow you?
6. Ready to lead. The definition of role model leadership: Be honest, sincere, lead by example, and practice what you preach.

Being a role model "can improve both the ethical climate and the internal work environment of an organization" (McMahone 2012). Leadership is a challenge, no doubt, but to truly create waves, change culture, and create a productive, high-performance environment, in which people can develop, every leader needs to start reflectively with him or herself and act as a role model to draw in followers.

As Derek Sivers (2010) so aptly puts it "the first follower is what transforms a lone nut into a leader." Without brave, mercurial followers, a leader remains a solitary stone-thrower with cooky ideas. But, without a role model, there are no followers. With followers; team members; those who have shared values, a leader is born. One of your greatest challenges in the near future will be to convince others of your drivers and philosophies, enter into discussion with high-potential colleagues, and to successfully share your vision and begin winning like-minded followers.

My management trainer colleague Lutz Pickhardt does a nice exercise with his participants, whereby he climbs onto a table, offers his hand to the nearest person, and invites them to join him on the table. There is often hesitation from the participant invited up onto the desk. Some completely refuse to climb up all together. Lutz jumps back down from the table and turns to the group and says:

You can ask someone to do something (get on the table). You can even make things as easy for them as you like (offer them a hand up), to help them join you. At the end of the day, though, the final choice lies with the person, whether they follow you or not.

Your job as a leader is to make that choice as easy as possible.

Chapter Leadership Challenge

Take a look at your group's culture. Put together a culture *pilot group*. Involve all levels of hierarchy in the discussion, from the CEO to the trainee. With this snapshot of the culture prevalent in your organization, ask the pilot group involved to envisage what kind of culture they would like to work in. Culture change can be slow, but the rewards can be paradigmatic.

By the same token, reflect on your team's own subculture, too. How do you do things in your team? The culture in your team may or may not be different from the organization's culture. Scrutinize the pros and cons of your group's subculture.

CHAPTER 12

What Is Next?

Do Not Be That Guy

So that is it. Those were the 11 most common mistakes that young leaders make, and some tips to avoid them. I hope that you have seen by now that leadership is not a toolbox that can be stocked with handy gizmos, gadgets, and devices to suddenly help you fix any managerial hiccup with some sort of magical wave of this leadership tool or that. Nor is there one defining list of characteristics that one requires in order to become an impactful leader of people. Leadership is the development of an antenna to *read* myriad business situations and use your honed instinct, supported by your reflected values, to make an honest, transparent decision, which you believe will lead to quality.

The vast majority of people who choose to leave their jobs do so not because of their tasks or responsibilities but because of their boss (Figure 12.1). Leaders are the reason why 75 percent of the people quit. We do not quit our jobs, we quit our bosses (Trupath 2015). Do not be that guy! Most of us have known or experienced poor leaders, leaders who did not motivate intrinsically, did not act as a role model, did not lead transformationally, and did not support in a strengths-oriented manner. Do you want one of my easiest leadership tips?

Do not be that guy!

Do not be the reason for your people to quit. It is mighty hard for us to change others, but we are in a position to develop ourselves every day. Work on yourself to become the leader you would like to become (not *that* guy).

Your Leadership Compass

Now that you have finished the book, I invite you to think about what comes next. Every day is a school day, and today is no different. To help

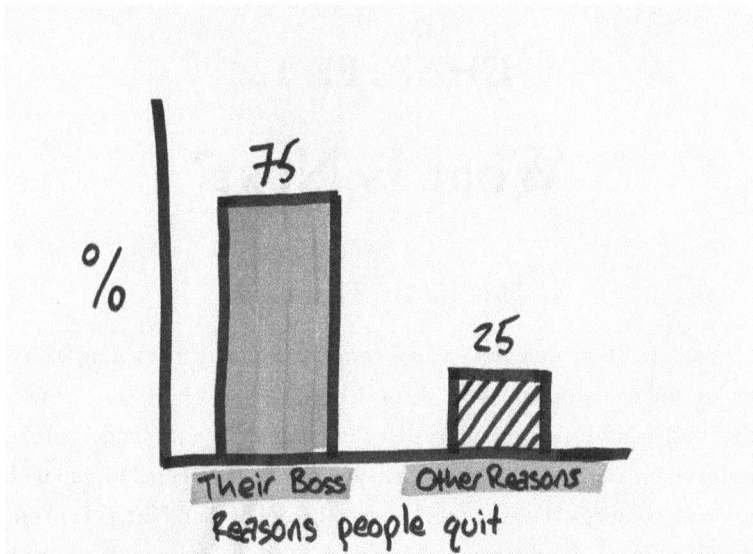

Figure 12.1 About 75 percent of the associates who quit their job do so because of their boss

you to continue your self-reflection, develop your own personal development project (PDP). Your PDP represents the areas of your leadership skill set upon which you would like to improve. Your PDP is not, for example, I would like to sell more products or I would like to get promoted at work. Your PDP is personal, related to your leadership and communication and is grounded in your values.

For the last time in this book (I promise), take a large piece of paper. Get yourself a bunch of magazines, newspapers, shots from the net or books, and trawl through until you find images that you would like to use in your collage. The images should represent your values, hopes, challenges, goals, strengths, and skills, and—combined—they defend your philosophy on leadership. This collage is your leadership compass, and you should return to it in sticky leadership times, when you need guidance or reminding of your leadership foundation. We ask our participants to create, present, and be proud of such collages at the end of almost all the young leader programs we deliver. It is the culmination of all your thoughts on leadership and you deserve to be very proud of it. Some of my participants have kindly allowed me to share their collages (Figures 12.2, 12.3, 12.4) with you to give you an idea of the kind of thing that you could create.

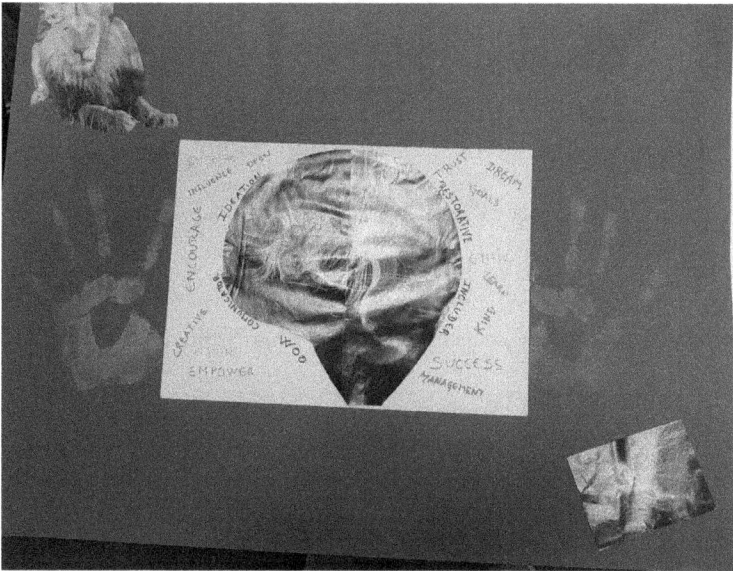

Figure 12.2 Leadership compass collage from Fernando M.

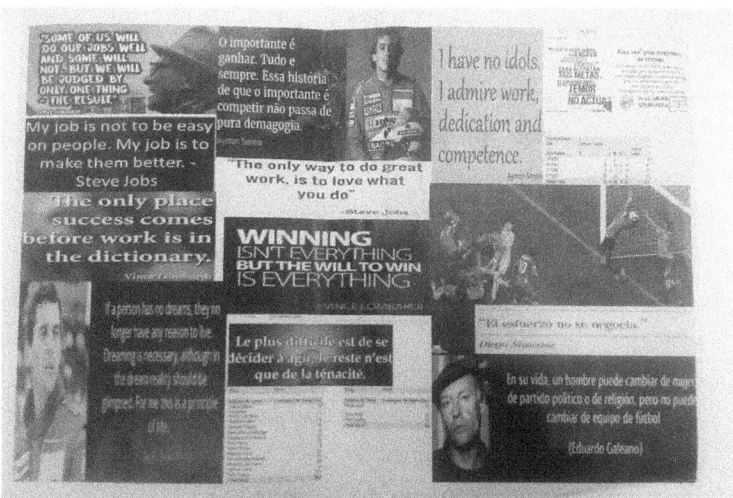

Figure 12.3 Leadership compass collage from Aldo O.

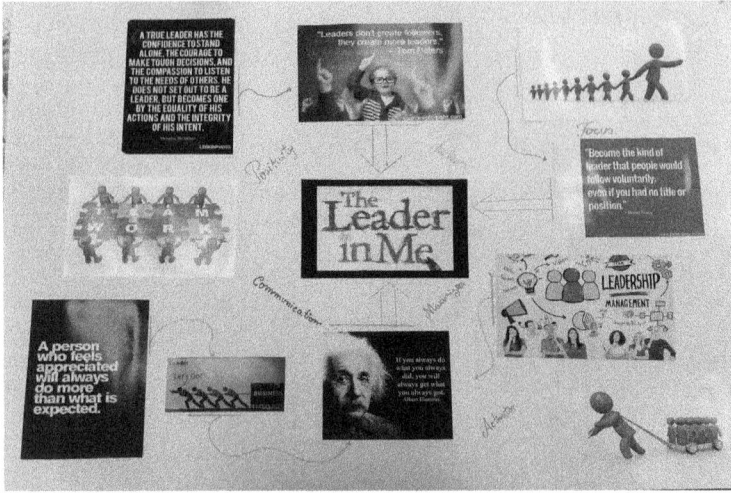

Figure 12.4 Leadership compass collage from Nancy S.

Change

And finally, what you are about to embark on is a not a leadership journey, it is a period of change. Every new project, in this case, your PDP, represents a change and understanding, and embracing change as an opportunity is essential for transformational, situational leaders.

When faced with a new, changing environment, such as a PDP, humans typically experience six stages (Figure 12.5) of mental reflection (Prochaska and Velicer 1997).

1. Precontemplation (resistance): No intention nor desire to change behavior
2. Contemplation (getting ready): Awareness of issue and need for change, but no commitment to engage
3. Preparation (ready): Intention to change behavior or to address the issue
4. Action: Conscious, implemented modification of behavior
5. Maintenance: The new behavior has now replaced the old, and changes needs to be sustained
6. Relapse: Behavior slips back into old patterns

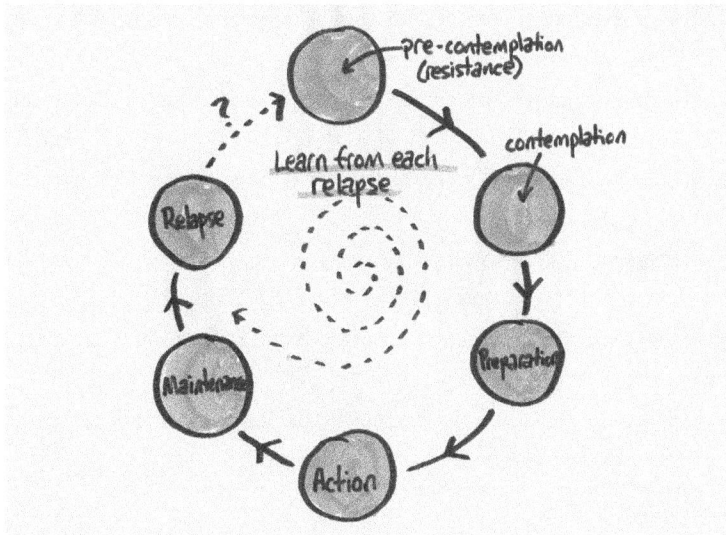

Figure 12.5 The stages of change

When faced with a change process (for example, your personal development), we often express resistance (precontemplation) at first. Things have functioned as they were. Why mess with the formula? After some research, coaching, and consideration, we often appreciate the potential of change and enter into the contemplation stage (contemplation), where we begin to consider our options and chances, without actually getting active. The click happens, when we decide to do something about it (preparation) and begin to plan our change strategy. Implementing that strategy or approach is known as the action phase (action). The final challenge for anyone wanting to realize genuine change in their life is to maintain the modification in behavior and make that the new normal (maintenance). Sadly, some slip back into old patterns (relapse), and as the diagram shows, this can send us back to the beginning of the loop. We now need to begin the whole process again to establish genuine change. It is important to remember that the loop is not uni-directional. People often jump up or down the stages before they develop a comfort zone for change. Such backward and forward motion in our acceptance of change is totally normal.

Take a moment to consider where you are right now, regarding your PDP, along the six stages of change. Are you sensing internal resistance to the impending change of role? Are you already preparing for the new paradigm of leadership or have you already taken action and implemented some cultural change? Whatever the status quo, regularly ask yourself what you need to advance to the next stage of change and jump to a lower stage of change to reappraise or start again. Change is constant, and change is fine. Change in ourselves can be frightening but it is what moves us to new achievements. Embrace it and strive to be a little better at what you do every day.

Driving the bus can be great fun. Good luck with it but remember, safety first. Do not forget to fasten your seatbelt.

References

Adamson, R.E. 1952. "Functional Fixedness as Related to Problem Solving: A Repetition of Three Experiments." *Journal of Experimental Psychology* 44, no. 4, p. 288.

Ait-Mokhtar, C. 2018. *Personal Communication*.

Albrecht, S.L., A.B. Bakker, J.A. Gruman, W.H. Macey, and A.M. Saks. 2015. "Employee Engagement, Human Resource Management Practices and Competitive Advantage: An integrated Approach." *Journal of Organizational Effectiveness: People and Performance* 2, no. 1, pp. 7–35.

Alderfer, C.P. 1969. "An Empirical Test of a New Theory of Human Needs." *Organizational Behavior and Human Performance* 4, no. 2, pp. 142–75.

Aldwin, C.M., H. Igarashi, D.F. Gilmer, and M.R. Levenson. 2017. *Health, Illness, and Optimal Aging: Biological and Psychosocial Perspectives*. Springer Publishing Company.

Amabile, T.M. 1996. *Creativity in Context: Update to the Social Psychology of Creativity*. Hachette, UK.

Anders, G. 2016. "Did Peter Drucker Actually Say 'Culture Eats Strategy for Breakfast'-and if so, where/when?" quora.com. https://quora.com/Did-Peter-Drucker-actually-say-culture-eats-strategy-for-breakfast-and-if-so-where-when (accessed July 07, 2018).

Anderson, N., K. KPotočnik, and J. Zhou. 2014. "Innovation and Creativity in Organizations: A State-of-the-Science Review, Prospective Commentary, and Guiding Framework." *Journal of Management* 40, no. 5, pp. 1297–333.

Anonymous. 2018. *Online Etymology Dictionary*. https://etymonline.com/word/stress (accessed June 07, 2018).

Anonymous. Transformational Leadership. Langston.edu. https://langston.edu/sites/default/files/basic-content-files/TransformationalLeadership.pdf (accessed June 09, 2018).

Ariely, D. 2008 "Whats the Value of a Big Bonus?" *New York Times*. https://nytimes.com/2008/11/20/opinion/20ariely.html (accessed June 09, 2018).

Ariely, D., U. Gneezy, G. Loewenstein, and N. Mazar. 2009. "Large Stakes and Big Mistakes." *The Review of Economic Studies* 76, no. 2, pp. 451–69.

Ariely, D., G. Loewenstein, and D. Prelec. 2006. "Tom Sawyer and the Construction of Value." *Journal of Economic Behavior & Organization* 60, no. 1, pp. 1–10.

Asch, S.E., and H. Guetzkow. 1951. "Effects of Group Pressure Upon the Modification and Distortion of Judgment." In *Groups, Leadership and Men*, 222–36. Pittsburgh, PA: Carnegie Press.

Asch, S.E. 1952. "Group Forces in the Modification and Distortion of Judgments." In *Social Psychology*, 450–501. Englewood Cliffs, NJ, US: Prentice-Hall, Inc.

Asch, S.E. 1956. "Studies of Independence and Conformity: I. A Minority of One Against a Unanimous Majority." *Psychological Monographs: General and Applied* 70, no. 9, pp. 1–70.

Asplund, J., J. Harter, S. Agrawal, and S. Plowman. 2016. "The Relationship Between Strengths-Based Employee Development and Organizational Outcomes." *Gallup*. https://static1.squarespace.com/static/ 577a17d9d482e9e2bce9bc68/t/58d4e81a20099e1b037cbced/1490348060 515/2015+Relationship+between+Strengths-based+employee+developmen t+and+organizational+outcomes+-+Gallup+StrengthsFinder+Singapore.pdf (accessed June 09, 2018).

Back, L. 2007. *The Art of Listening*. Berg.

Bakker, A.B., and P.L. Costa. 2014. "Chronic Job Burnout and Daily Functioning: A Theoretical Analysis." *Burnout Research* 1, no. 3, pp. 112–19.

Baldwin, C., and A. Linnea. 2010. *The Circle Way: A Leader in Every Chair*. Berrett-Koehler Publishers.

Barnes, C.M., L. Lucianetti, D.P. Bhave, and M.S. Christian. 2015. "You Wouldn't Like Me When I'm Sleepy: Leaders' Sleep, Daily Abusive Supervision, and Work Unit Engagement." *Academy of Management Journal* 58, no. 5, pp. 1419–37.

Bass, B.M. 1985. *Leadership and Performance Beyond Expectations*. New York, NY: Free Press.

Bass, B.M. 1995. "Theory of Transformational Leadership Redux." *The Leadership Quarterly* 6, no. 4, pp. 463–78.

Bass, B.M., and R.E. Riggio. 2006. *Transformational Leadership*. Psychology Press.

Bassett, L. 2014. "What is Stress." Slideshare.net. https://de.slideshare.net/ midwestcenter/what-is-stress-and-its-signs-causes-effects-and-effective-management (accessed June 09, 2018).

Bennett, N., and G.J. Lemoine. 2014. "What a Difference a Word Makes: Understanding Threats to Performance in a VUCA World." *Business Horizons* 57, no. 3, pp. 311–17.

Betz, W. 1959. "Lehnwörter und Lehnprägungen im Vor- und Frühdeutschen." In *Deutsche Wortgeschichte*, eds. F. Maurer and F. Stroh, 2nd ed. vol. 1, 127–47. Berlin: Schmidt.

Bodie, G.D., A.J. Vickery, K. Cannava, and S.M. Jones. 2015. "The Role of 'Active Listening' In Informal Helping Conversations: Impact on Perceptions of Listener Helpfulness, Sensitivity, and Supportiveness and Discloser Emotional Improvement." *Western Journal of Communication* 79, no. 2, pp. 151–73.

Bond, M.H. 1991. "Chinese Values and Health: A Cultural-level Examination." *Psychology and Health* 5, no. 2, pp. 137–52.

Bond, R., and P.B. Smith. 1996. "Culture and Conformity: A Meta-analysis of Studies Using Asch's (1952b, 1956) Line Judgment Task." *Psychological Bulletin* 119, no. 1, p. 111.

Bostrom, R., and C. Bryant. 1980. "Factors in the Retention of Information Presented Orally: The Role of Short-term Listening." *Western Journal of Communication* (Includes Communication Reports) 44, no. 2, pp. 137–45.

Bransford, J. D., Brown, A. L., & Cocking, R. R. (2000). How People Learn: Brain, Mind, Experience, and School. Washington DC: National Academy Press.

Browson, T. 2010. "What Is Reframing?" Adaringadventure.com. https://adaringadventure.com/whats-reframing/ (accessed June 09, 2018).

Buckingham, M., and D.O. Clifton. 2001. *Now, Discover your Strengths*. Simon & Schuster.

Buckingham, M., and C. Coffman. 2014. *First, Break All the Rules: What the World's Greatest Managers do Differently*. Simon & Schuster.

Burns, J.M. 1978. *Leadership*. New York, NY: Harper and Row.

Cave, A. 2017. "Culture Eats Strategy For Breakfast. So What's For Lunch?" Forbes.com. https://forbes.com/sites/andrewcave/2017/11/09/culture-eats-strategy-for-breakfast-so-whats-for-lunch/#138e35287e0f (July 13, 2018).

Chron. http://smallbusiness.chron.com/transformational-leadership-vs-transactional-leadership-definition-13834.html (June 09, 2018).

Cialdini, R. 2006 . " Influence, Harper Business; Revised edition."

Cialdini, R. 2012. "Science of Persuasion." Youtube.com. https://youtube.com/watch?v=cFdCzN7Rybw (July 13, 2018).

Clay, R. 2011. "Stressed in America." *American Psychological Association*. http://apa.org/monitor/2011/01/stressed-america.aspx (June 09, 2018).

Clifton, D.O., and J.K. Harter. 2003. "Investing in Strengths." In *Positive Organizational Scholarship: Foundations of a New Discipline*, eds. A. Cameron, B. Dutton, and C. Quinn, 111–21. San Francisco: Berrett-Koehler Publishers.

Conger, J.A., and R.N. Kanungo. 1998. *Charismatic Leadership in Organizations*. Thousand Oaks, CA: Sage.

Cooperatives UK. 2015. "The Co-operative Economy 2015."

Dahl, R. 2003. *The Twits*. Dramatic Publishing.

Daily Mail. n.d. "Concorde Tickets Snapped Up." Dailymail.co.uk. http://dailymail.co.uk/news/article-196994/Concorde-tickets-snapped-up.html (accessed June 09, 2018).

Dantzer, R., J.C. O'Connor, G.G. Freund, R.W. Johnson, and K.W. Kelley. 2008. "From Inflammation to Sickness and Depression: When the Immune System Subjugates the Brain." *Nature Reviews Neuroscience* 9, no. 1, pp. 46–56.

De Bono, E. 2017. *Six Thinking Hats*. London, UK: Penguin.

Daum, A. 2003. *Kennedy in Berlin, Politik, Kultur und Öffentlichkeit im Kalten Krieg*. Paderborn: Ferdinand Schöningh Verlag.

Demirdöğen, Ü.D. 2010. "The Roots of Research in (political) Persuasion: Ethos, Pathos, Logos and the Yale Studies of Persuasive Communications." *International Journal of Social Inquiry* 3, no. 1, pp. 189–201.

Dempster, D. 2012. "Are you in Threat Mode? 6 Tools To Stop the Yelling." Impact ADHD.com. https://impactadhd.com/manage-emotions-and-impulses/are-you-in-threat-mode-6-tools-to-stop-the-yelling/ (accessed July 13, 2018)

Dubrin, A. 2007. *Leadership: Research Findings, Practice, and Skills*. New York, NY: Houghton Mifflin.

Duncker, K., and L.S. Lees. 1945. "On problem-solving." *Psychological Monographs* 58, no. 5, p. i.

Dürrbeck, K. 2018. *Personal Communication*.

Echevarria, M. 2008 "20 Best Foreign Loanwords in English." Altalang.com. https://altalang.com/beyond-words/2008/11/17/20-best-foreign-loanwords-in-english (June 09, 2018).

Eisenhower, R., and L. Shanock. 2003. "Rewards, Intrinsic Motivation, and Creativity: A Case Study of Conceptual and Methodological Isolation." *Creativity Research Journal* 15, nos. 2–3, pp. 121–30.

Ekman, P., W.V. Friesen, M. O'sullivan, A. Chan, I. Diacoyanni-Tarlatzis, K. Heider, and K. Scherer. 1987. "Universals and Cultural Differences in the Judgments of Facial Expressions of Emotion." *Journal of Personality and Social Psychology* 53, no. 4, p. 712.

Fabritius, F., and H.W. Hagemann. 2017. *The Leading Brain: Powerful Science-based Strategies for Achieving Peak Performance*. London, UK: Penguin.

Freedman, J. L., & Fraser, S. C. 1966. Compliance without Pressure: The Foot-in-the-door Technique. *Journal of personality and social psychology*, 4(2), 195.

Freese, J.H. 1926. *Aristotle: The Art of Rhetoric*. Loeb Classical Library.

Myerson, A., FRIENDS, 1:15. "The One with the Stoned Guy." directed by Alison Myerson, aired 2/16/95, on NBC, http://friends-tv.org/zz115.html

Guardian 2007. "And Materazzi's exact words to Zidane were..." https://web.archive.org/web/20070821090226/http://football.guardian.co.uk/News_Story/0%2C%2C2151641%2C00.html (accessed July 13, 2018).

Gallup Organization. 2018. Gallupstrengthscenter.com (accessed June 09, 2018).

Gallup Organization. 2001. Summary of Selection Research Item Bank. Internal Company Database.

Gallup Organization. 2002. *Workplace Poll*. Internal Research Document.

Geldard, K., and D. Geldard. 1998. *Counselling Children: A Practical Introduction*. London: Sage.

Gilliard, M. n.d. "Bill Gates Leadership Style." Leadership and Development. com. https://leadership-and-development.com/bill-gates-leadership-style/ (accessed June 09, 2018).

Glock, J.W. 1955. *The Relative Value of Three Methods of Improving Reading: Tachistoscope, Films, and Determined Effort* [PhD thesis]. University of Nebraska-Lincoln.

Glucksberg, S. 1962. "The Influence of Strength of Drive on Functional Fixedness and Perceptual Recognition." *Journal of Experimental Psychology* 63, no. 1, p. 36.

Glucksberg, S. 1964. "Problem Solving: Response Competition and the Influence of Drive." *Psychological Reports* 15, no. 3, pp. 939–42.

Glucksberg, S., and R.W. Weisberg. 1966. "Verbal Behavior and Problem Solving: Some Effects of Labeling in a Functional Fixedness Problem." *Journal of Experimental Psychology* 71, no. 5, p. 659.

Gneezy, U., and A. Rustichini. 2000. "A Fine is a Price." *The Journal of Legal Studies* 29, no. 1, pp. 1–17.

Goffee, R., and G. Jones. 2006. *Why Should Anyone be Led by You?: What It Takes to Be an Authentic Leader.* Harvard Business Press.

Gordon, T. 2008. *Parent Effectiveness Training: The Proven Program for Raising Responsible Children.* Harmony.

Graeff, C.L. 1983. "The Situational Leadership Theory: A Critical View." *Academy of Management Review* 8, no. 2, pp. 285–91.

Gumusluoglu, L., and A. Ilsev. 2009. "Transformational Leadership, Creativity, and Organizational Innovation." *Journal of Business Research* 62, no. 4, pp. 461–73.

Hagemann, H. 2018. *Personal Communication.*

Hahnke, E. 2017. "Feedback Geben?" Kein Problem!. tbd.community. https:// tbd.community/de/a/konstruktives-feedback-wahrnehmung-wirkung-wunsch (accessed June 09, 2018).

Harari, Y. N. 2014. *Sapiens: A Brief History of Humankind.* Random House.

Harter, J.K., and F.L. Schmidt. 2002. "Employee Engagement, Satisfaction, and Business Unit-level Outcomes: Meta-analysis." *Gallup Technical Report.*

Harter, J.K., F.L. Schmidt, and T.L. Hayes. 2002. "Business-unit-level Relationship Between Employee Satisfaction, Employee Engagement, and Business Outcomes: A Meta-analysis." *Journal of Applied Psychology* 87, no. 2, p. 268.

Hattie, J. 2008. *Visible Learning: A Synthesis of Over 800 Meta-Analyses Relating to Achievement.* New York, NY: Routledge.

Heath, C., and D. Heath. 2007. *Made to Stick: Why Some Ideas Survive and Others Die.* Random House.

Heinrich Heine Universität. https://phil-fak.uni-duesseldorf.de/fileadmin/
Redaktion/Institute/Sozialwissenschaften/BF/Barz/Aktuelles/2012_Forsa-
Studie_Studentenalltag_in_NRW.pdf (accessed June 09, 2018).

Henson, R. 2011. "The Leadership of Steve Jobs." Rutgers Business School.
http://business.rutgers.edu/business-insights/leadership-steve-jobs (accessed
June 09, 2018).

Hersey, P., and K.H. Blanchard. 1977. *Situational Leadership*. California
American University, Center for Leadership Studies.

Hey-che.com. 2017. "Che Guevara Quotes, Phrases, Citations and Sayings."
Hey-che.com. http://hey-che.com/famous-quotes-from-el-che-guevara/
(accessed July 13, 2018).

Higgins, C., and R. Walker. 2010. "Strategies of Persuasion in Social/
Environmental Reporting," In *APIRA 2010: Proceedings of the 6th Asia
Pacific Interdisciplinary Research in Accounting Conference*, 1–24. University
of Sydney.

Hofstede, G. 1991. *Cultures and Organizations: Software of the Mind*. London:
McGraw-Hill.

Hofstede, G., and M. Minkov. 2010. "Long-versus Short-term Orientation: New
Perspectives." *Asia Pacific Business Review* 16, no. 4, pp. 493–504.

Ingram, D. 2018. "Transformational Leadership Vs. Transactional Leadership
Definition."

Irlenbusch, B. 2009. "When Performance-related Pay Backfires." London
School of Economics. http://lse.ac.uk/website-archive/newsAndMedia/news/
archives/2009/06/performancepay.aspx (accessed June 09, 2018).

Isaacson, W. 2011. *Steve Jobs*. New York, NY: Simon & Schuster.

Isaacson, W. 2012. "The Real Leadership Lessons of Steve Jobs." *Harvard Business
Review* 90, no. 4, pp. 92–102.

Joyce, P.R., R.T. Mulder, and C.R. Cloninger. 1994. "Temperament and
Hypercortisolemia in Depression." *American Journal of Psychiatry* 151, no. 2,
pp. 195–98.

Jenewein, W. 2008." Das Klinsmann Projekt." *Harvard Business Manager*.
https://fhsg.ch/fhs.nsf/files/ifu_StU_Publikationen_Betriebswirtschaft%20
f%C3%BCr%20F%C3%BChrungskr%C3%A4fte_Lehrmaterialien_
Kapitel%206_Das%20Klinsmann-Projekt/$FILE/Artikel_06_08_
Harvard%20Business%20Manager_Das%20Klinsmann-Projekt.pdf
(accessed July 13, 2018).

Judge, T.A., and R.F. Piccolo. 2004. "Transformational and Transactional
Leadership: A Meta-analytic Test of their Relative Validity." *Journal of Applied
Psychology* 89, no. 5, p. 755.

Jung, D.I., C. Chow, and A. Wu. 2003. "The Role of Transformational Leadership
in Enhancing Organizational Innovation: Hypotheses and Some Preliminary
Findings." *The Leadership Quarterly* 14, nos. 4–5, pp. 525–44.

Kaluza, G. 2018. *Stressbewältigung: Trainingsmanual zur psychologischen Gesundheitsförderung*. Springer-Verlag.

Kasser, T., and R.M. Ryan. 1993. "A Dark Side of the American Dream: Correlates of Financial Success as a Central Life Aspiration." *Journal of Personality and Social Psychology* 65, no. 2, p. 410.

Kirkland, R. 2009. *What Matters? Ten Questions That Will Shape Our Future*, 80. McKinsey Management Institute.

Knieling, M. 2018. *Personal Communication*.

Kouzes, J.M. and B.Z. Posner. 1995. *The Leadership Challenge*. San Francisco: Jossey-Bass.

Kouzes, J.M., and B.Z. Posner. 2010. *The Truth About Leadership*. Sound view Executive Book Summaries.

Kruse, K. 2012. "100 Best Quotes On Leadership." Forbes.com. https://forbes.com/sites/kevinkruse/2012/10/16/quotes-on-leadership/#70669c3a2feb (accessed June 09, 2018).

Lazear, E. 2000. "The Peter Principle: Promotions and Declining Productivity." Semantic Scholar. https://pdfs.semanticscholar.org/2d12/ccf76e4cc072708 5078a637a6290e12aef49.pdf (June 09, 2018).

Lee, D., and D. Hatesohl. 1993. "Listening: Our Most Used Communications Skill." University of Missouri. https://extension2.missouri.edu/cm150 (accessed June 09, 2018).

Lemyre, P.N., D.C. Treasure, and G.C. Roberts. 2006. "Influence of Variability in Motivation and Affect on Elite Athlete Burnout Susceptibility." *Journal of Sport and Exercise Psychology* 28, no. 1, pp. 32–48.

Liebnau, D. 2018. *Personal Communication*.

Lipman, V. 2018. "Management Is 10% Work And 90% People." Forbes.com. https://forbes.com/sites/victorlipman/2018/03/02/management-is-10-work-and-90-people/#1f2502986f0c (accessed July 16, 2018).

Loehr, J.E., and T. Schwartz. 2005. *The Power of Full Engagement: Managing Energy, Not Time, is the Key to High Performance and Personal Renewal*. Simon & Schuster.

Lorenzen, C. 2018. *Personal Communication*.

Lowther, D. 2013. "Brilliant Minds Blog: Neurological Levels." https://youtube.com/watch?v=xb9hUFIaf-Q (July 13, 2018).

Lupien, S.J., M. De Leon, S. De Santi, A. Convit, C. Tarshish, N.P.V. Nair, and M.J. Meaney. 1998. "Cortisol Levels During Human Aging Predict Hippocampal Atrophy and Memory Deficits." *Nature Neuroscience* 1, no. 1, p. 69.

Luthans, F. 2002. "The Need for and Meaning of Positive Organizational Behavior." *Journal of Organizational Behavior* 23, no. 6, pp. 695–706.

Luthans, F. 2011. *Organizational Behavior: An Evidence-based Approach*, 12th ed. New York, NY: McGraw-Hill/Irwin.

Luthans, F., C.M. Youssef, and B.J. Avolio. 2007. *Psychological Capital: Developing the Human Competitive Edge.* Oxford: Oxford University Press.

Manges, K., J. Scott-Cawiezell, and M.M. Ward. January 2017. "Maximizing Team Performance: The Critical Role of the Nurse Leader." In *Nursing Forum* 52, no. 1, pp. 21–29.

Martínez Sánchez, A., M. Pérez Pérez, P. de Luis Carnicer, and M. José Vela Jiménez. 2007. "Teleworking and Workplace Flexibility: A Study of Impact on Firm Performance." *Personnel Review* 36, no. 1, pp. 42–64.

Marzano, R., D. Pickering, and J. Pollock. 2001. *Classroom Instruction that Works: Research-based Strategies for Increasing Student Achievement.* Alexandria, VA: ASCD.

Maslow, A.H. 1971. *The Farther Reaches of Human Nature.* Arkana/Penguin Books.

McClelland, D.C. 1951. "Measuring Motivation in Phantasy: The Achievement Motive." In *Groups, Leadership and Men; Research in Human Relations*, ed. H. Guetzkow, 191–205. Oxford, England: Carnegie Press.

McMahone, M. 2012. "Servant Leadership as a Teachable Ethical Concept." *American Journal of Business Education* (Online) 5, no. 3, p. 339.

Mehrabian, A., and M. Wiener. 1967. "Decoding of Inconsistent Communications." *Journal of Personality and Social Psychology* 6, no. 1, p. 109.

Mehrabian, A., and S. Ferris. 1967. "Inference of Attitudes from Nonverbal Communication in Two Channels." *Journal of Consulting and Clinical Psychology* 31, no. 3, pp. 248–52.

Melamed, S., U. Ugarten, A. Shirom, L. Kahana, Y. Lerman, and P. Froom, 1999. "Chronic Burnout, Somatic Arousal and Elevated Salivary Cortisol Levels." *Journal of Psychosomatic Research* 46, no. 6, pp. 591–98.

Merg, K., and T. Knödler. 2005." Überleben im Job." *Berufsalltag ohne Stress und Burn-out/Coaching für die Karriere/Umgang mit Chefs und Kollegen.* Frankfurt/M: Redline Wirtschaft.

Milgram, S. 1963. "Behavioral Study of Obedience." *The Journal of Abnormal and Social Psychology* 67, no. 4, pp. 371–78.

Morieux, Y. 2015. "How too Many Rules Keep You From Getting Things Done." [Video file]. https://ted.com/talks/yves_morieux_how_too_many_rules_at_work_keep_you_from_getting_things_done (accessed June 09, 2018).

Morningstar, J.A. 2012. "Drives, Performance, Creativity and Introversion in the Workplace." MPRA. https://mpra.ub.uni-muenchen.de/62939/1/MPRA_paper_62939.pdf (accessed June 09, 2018).

Murray, H.A. 1938. *Explorations in Personality.* New York, NY: Oxford University Press.

National Research Council. 2000. *How People Learn: Brain, Mind, Experience, and School: Expanded Edition.* National Academies Press.

Newton, L. 1990. *Overconfidence in the Communication of Intent: Heard and Unheard Melodies* [PhD. dissertation]. Stanford University.

Nichols, R.G., and L.A. Stevens. 1957. *Are You Listening?* 4–6. New York, NY: McGraw-Hill.

Nishiyama, K., and J.V. Johnson. 1997. "Karoshi—Death from Overwork: Occupational Health Consequences of Japanese Production Management." *International Journal of Health Services* 27, no. 4, pp. 625–41.

Northouse, P.G. 2007. *Leadership: Theory and Practice*, 4th ed. Thousand Oaks, CA: Sage.

Ogata, N. 2001. "A Type Theory for Typing, Meta-Typing, and Ontological Information in Discourse." In *Fourth International Workshop on Computational Semantics*, pp. 10–12.

Oster, S. 2014, "Is Work Killing You?" Bloomberg.com. https://bloomberg.com/news/articles/2014-06-29/is-work-killing-you-in-china-workers-die-at-their-desks (accessed June 09, 2018).

Park, J. 2016. "The Dangers of Overwork are Becoming Widespread." FinancialTimes.com. https://ft.com/content/4be46aa6-9ad2-11e6-8f9b-70e3cabccfae (accessed June 09, 2018).

Pelleymounter, M.A., M.J. Cullen, and C.L. Wellman. 1995. "Characteristics of BDNF-induced Weight Loss." *Experimental Neurology* 131, no. 2, pp. 229–38.

Petersen, C. 2013 "Seven Tips for Giving Feedback to Others." *Insights by Stanford Business*. https://gsb.stanford.edu/insights/carole-robin-feedback-gift (accessed June 09, 2018).

Pink, D. 2010. "The Autonomous Work Space." Forbes.com. https://forbes.com/2010/04/29/best-buy-office-opinions-workspaces-daniel-pink.html#5bfccace795e (accessed June 09, 2018)

Pink, D.H. 2011. *Drive: The Surprising Truth About What Motivates Us.* Canongate Books. Kindle Edition.

Pinker, S. 2003. *The Language Instinct: How the Mind Creates Language.* London, UK: Penguin.

Prochaska, J.O., and W.F. Velicer. 1997. "The Transtheoretical Model of Health Behavior Change." *American Journal of Health Promotion* 12, no. 1, pp. 38–48.

Provan, J. 2013. *Ich bin ein Berliner.* John, F. *Kennedys Deutschlandbesuch* 1963. Berlin- Berlin, Story-Verlag.

Rampton, J. 2016. "How Bill Gates Became a Leadership Legend." Entrepreneur.com. https://entrepreneur.com/article/250607 (accessed June 09, 2018).

Rath, T., and B. Conchie. 2008. *Strengths Based Leadership: Great leaders, Teams, and Why People Follow.* Simon & Schuster.

Regan, D.T. 1971. "Effects of a Favor and Liking on Compliance." *Journal of Experimental Social Psychology* 7, no. 6, pp. 627–39.

Reiss, S. 2004. "Multifaceted Nature of Intrinsic Motivation: The Theory of 16 Basic Desires." *Review of General Psychology* 8, no. 3, p. 179.

Riggio, R. 2009. "Are You a Transformational Leader?" Psychology Today. https://psychologytoday.com/intl/blog/cutting-edge-leadership/200903/are-you-transformational-leader (accessed June 09, 2018).

Robert, C. 2018. "Principals of Persuasion." Influence at work.com https://influenceatwork.com/principles-of-persuasion/ (accessed June 09, 2018).

Rogers, C.R., and R.E. Farson. 1957. *Active Listening*. Industrial Relations Center of the University of Chicago.

Rose, T. 2017. *The End of Average: How to Succeed in a World That Values Sameness*. London, UK: Penguin.

Rosenzweig, P. 2014. *The Halo Effect:... and the Eight Other Business Delusions that Deceive Managers*. Simon & Schuster.

Roth, C. 2017. "Why Henry Ford's Most Famous Quote Is Dead Wrong." Entrepreneur.com. https://entrepreneur.com/article/290410 (accessed June 09, 2018). (Henry Ford quote)

Ryan, L. 2018. "Ten Business Buzzwords That Make You Sound Like An Idiot." Forbes.com. https://forbes.com/sites/lizryan/2018/01/05/ten-business-buzzwords-that-make-you-sound-like-an-idiot/#2cf8dcab68ed (accessed June 09, 2018).

Ryan, R.M., and E.L. Deci. 2000. "Self-determination Theory and the Facilitation of Intrinsic Motivation, Social Development, and Well-being." *American psychologist* 55, no. 1, p. 68.

Saks, A.M. 2006. "Antecedents and Consequences of Employee Engagement." *Journal of managerial psychology* 21, no. 7, pp. 600–19.

Schürmann, P. 2018. *Personal Communication*.

Schilling, D. 2012. "10 Steps To Effective Listening." Forbes.com. https://forbes.com/sites/womensmedia/2012/11/09/10-steps-to-effective-listening/#1dcf859d3891 (accessed June 09, 2018).

Schmidt, F.L., and J. Rauschenberger. April 1986. "Utility analysis for Practitioners." Paper presented at the First Annual Conference of the Society for Industrial and Organizational Psychology, Chicago.

Schmidt, F.L., J.E. Hunter, R.C. McKenzie, and T.W. Muldrow. 1979." Impact of Valid Selection Procedures on Work-force Productivity." *Journal of Applied Psychology* 64, no. 6, 609–26.

Schramm, W. 1954. "How Communication Works." In *The Process and Effects of Communication*, ed. W.U. Schramm, 3–26. Illinois: University of Illinois Press.

Schürmann, P. 2018. *Personal Communication*.

Searle, J.R. 1985. *Expression and Meaning: Studies in the Theory of Speech Acts*. Cambridge: University Press.

Seligman, M.E., and M. Csikszentmihalyi. 2000. "Positive Psychology: An Introduction." *American Psychological Association* 55, no. 1, p. 5.

Seligman, M.E.P. 1998. "Positive Social Sciences." *APA Monitor* 29, no. 4, pp. 2–5.

Seligman, M.E.P. 1994. *What You Can Change and What you can't.* New York, NY: Knopf.

Seligman, M.E.P. 1999. *Positive Psychology. Presidential Address Delivered at the 107 Convention of the American Psychological Association.* Boston.

Shannon, C.E., and W. Weaver. 1949. *The Mathematical Theory of Communication.* Urbana, Illinois: University of Illinois Press.

Sharpe, S., and H. Cowie. 1998. *Counselling and Supporting Children in Distress.* London: Sage.

Sheline, Y.I., P.W. Wang, M.H. Gado, J.G. Csernansky, and M.W. Vannier. 1996. "Hippocampal Atrophy in Recurrent Major Depression." *Proceedings of the National Academy of Sciences* 93, no. 9, pp. 3908–13.

Sinek, S. 2009. *Start with Why: How Great Leaders Inspire Everyone to Take Action.* London, UK: Penguin.

Sivers, D. 2010. "How to Start a Movement." TED.com. https://ted.com/talks/derek_sivers_how_to_start_a_movement/transcript (accessed June 09, 2018).

Sosik, J.J. 2005. "The Role of Personal Values in the Charismatic Leadership of Corporate Managers: A Model and Preliminary Field Study." *The Leadership Quarterly* 16, no. 2, pp. 221–44.

Stanford University. 2010. "Aristotle's Rhetoric." Stanford Encyclodaedia of Philosophy. https://plato.stanford.edu/entries/aristotle-rhetoric/#Bib (accessed June 09, 2018).

Statistics Canada. 2015. "Selected Characteristics of Employed Adults Aged 20 to 64 Reporting Higher Levels of Stress, by Main Source of Stress, 2010."

Statistics Canada. https://statcan.gc.ca/pub/11-008-x/2011002/t/11562/tbl02-eng.htm (accessed June 09, 2018).

Stock-Homburg, R. 2009. " Der Zusammenhang zwischen Mitarbeiter- und Kundenzufriedenheit." *Direkte, indirekte und moderierende Effekte.* Heidelberg: Springer.

Stogdill, R.M. 1974. *Handbook of Leadership: A Survey of Theory and Research.* New York, NY: The Free Press.

Story, M. 2016. "5 Levels of High Impact Delegation." Mack Story.com http://mackstory.com/2014/12/31/5-levels-of-high-impact-delegation/ (accessed June 09, 2018).

Strohmetz, D.B., B. Rind, R. Fisher, and M. Lynn. 2002. " Sweetening the Till: The Use of Candy to Increase Restaurant Tipping." *Journal of Applied Social Psychology* 32, no. 2, pp. 300–09.

Suvorov, A. 2003. "Addiction to Rewards." Presentation delivered at the European Winter Meeting of the Econometric Society, October 25, 2013.

Taylor, T., & Booth-Butterfield, S. 1993. Getting a Foot in the Door with Drinking and Driving: A Field Study of Healthy Influence. *Communication Research Reports, 10*(1), 95-101.

Techniker Krankenkasse. 2012. "TK-Stress-Studie NRW-Studenten 2012 Ergebnisse einer repräsentativen Forsa-Umfrage aus Mai 201."

Ten Brummelhuis, L.L., C.L. Ter Hoeven, A.B. Bakker, and B. Peper. 2011." Breaking Through the Loss Cycle of Burnout: The Role of Motivation." *Journal of Occupational and Organizational Psychology* 84, no. 2, pp. 268–87.

Tosey, P., and J. Mathison. 2003. "Neuro-linguistic Programming and Learning Theory: A Response." *The Curriculum Journal* 14, no. 3, pp. 371–88.

Trupath. 2015. "20 Company Culture Stats You Need To Know." Blog. trupathresearch.com. http://blog.trupathsearch.com/company-culture-stats (accessed July 13, 2018).

Tuckman, B.W. 1965. "Developmental Sequence in Small Groups." *Psychological Bulletin* 63, no. 6, p. 384.

Tuckman, B.W., and M.A.C. Jensen. 1977. "Stages of Small-group Development Revisited." *Group & Organization Studies* 2, no. 4, pp. 419–27.

Van Vugt, M., R. Hogan, and R.B. Kaiser. 2008. "Leadership, Followership, and Evolution: Some Lessons from the Past." *American Psychologist* 63, no. 3, 182–96.

Villar, F. 2007. "Intergenerational or Multigenerational? A Question of Nuance." *Journal of Intergenerational Relationships* 5, no. 1, pp. 115–17.

Wang, G., I.S. Oh, S.H. Courtright, and A.E. Colbert. 2011. "Transformational Leadership and Performance Across Criteria and Levels: A Meta-analytic Review of 25 Years of Research." *Group & Organization Management* 36, no. 2, pp. 223–70.

Wayshack, M. 2014. "Closing More Sales." Markwayshack.com. https://marcwayshak.com/closing-more-sales/ (accessed June 09, 2018).

Webster, V., and M. Webster. 2018. "How to Be a Good Leadership Role Model." Leadership Thoughts. https://leadershipthoughts.com/leader-are-you-a-role-model/ (accessed June 09, 2018).

Wieman, C.E. 2007. "The 'Curse of Knowledge' or Why Intuition About Teaching Often Fails." *American Physical Society News* 16, no. 10.

Wiggins, G. 2012. "Seven Keys to Effective Feedback." In *On Formative Assessment: Readings from Educational Leadership*, ed. M. Scherer. Alexandria: ASCD.

Winne, P.H., and A.F. Hadwin. 2008. "The Weave of Motivation and Self-regulated Learning." In *Motivation and Self-regulated Learning: Theory, Research, and Applications*, eds. D. Schunk and B. Zimmerman. Routledge.

Wrangham, R.W., and D. Peterson. 1996. *Demonic Males: Apes and the Origins of Human Violence*. Houghton Mifflin Harcourt.

www.Uk.coop. https://uk.coop/sites/default/files/uploads/attachments/co-op_economy_2015.pdf (accessed June 09, 2018).

Yukl, G. 2006. *Leadership in Organizations*, 6th ed. Upper Saddle River, NJ: Pearson-Prentice Hall.

About the Author

Matt L. Beadle is a British management consultant who specializes in leadership development for young and new managers. After completing bachelor's and master's degrees at Greenwich and Birmingham City universities, respectively, Matt became a serial entrepreneur, setting up and running several companies before the sale of the last one in 2016. Since 2000 he has worked as a freelance management trainer and facilitator for Fortune 500 companies and global players across the world. He has trained or moderated over 20,000 executives of 40 different nationalities in over 20 countries and is one of the most renowned leadership experts working out of mainland Europe today.

Matt's unique brand of humorous, energetic training and moderation inspires his participants and no two workshops are the same. Matt is married and lives together with his wife and their two children in Werther, Germany (where the famous sweets come from). Matt is the author of two other books, and produces his own leadership video courses, available on the Internet.

Index

OTHER TITLES IN THE HUMAN RESOURCE MANAGEMENT AND ORGANIZATIONAL BEHAVIOR COLLECTION

- *Conflict and Leadership: How to Harness the Power of Conflict to Create Better Leaders and Build Thriving Teams* by Christian Muntean
- *Creating the Accountability Culture: The Science of Life Changing Leadership* by Yvonnne Thompson
- *Managing Organizational Change: The Measurable Benefits of Applied iOCM* by Linda C. Mattingly
- *Lead Self First Before Leading Others: A Life Planning Resource* by Stephen K. Hacker and Marvin Washington
- *The HOW of Leadership: Inspire People to Achieve Extraordinary Results* by Maxwell Ubah
- *Leading the High-Performing Company: A Transformational Guide to Growing Your Business and Outperforming Your Competition* by Heidi Pozzo
- *The Concise Coaching Handbook: How to Coach Yourself and Others to Get Business Results* by Elizabeth Dickinson
- *How Successful Engineers Become Great Business Leaders* by Paul Rulkens
- *Redefining Competency Based Education: Competence for Life* by Nina Jones Morel and Bruce Griffiths
- *From Behind the Desk to the Front of the Stage: How to Enhance Your Presentation Skills* by David Worsfold

Announcing the Business Expert Press Digital Library

Concise e-books business students need for classroom and research

This book can also be purchased in an e-book collection by your library as

- a one-time purchase,
- that is owned forever,
- allows for simultaneous readers,
- has no restrictions on printing, and
- can be downloaded as PDFs from within the library community.

Our digital library collections are a great solution to beat the rising cost of textbooks. E-books can be loaded into their course management systems or onto students' e-book readers.
The **Business Expert Press** digital libraries are very affordable, with no obligation to buy in future years. For more information, please visit **www.businessexpertpress.com/librarians**. To set up a trial in the United States, please email **sales@businessexpertpress.com**.

www.ingramcontent.com/pod-product-compliance
Lightning Source LLC
Chambersburg PA
CBHW060603210326
41519CB00014B/3553